Maulana Daud's *Cāndāyan*

A CRITICAL STUDY

Maulana Daud's *Cāndāyan*

A CRITICAL STUDY

NASEEM A. HINES

MANOHAR
2009

First published 2009

ISBN 81-7304-728-6

Published by

Ajay Kumar Jain for
Manohar Publishers & Distributors
4753/23 Ansari Road, Daryaganj
New Delhi 110002

Typeset by

Guru Typograph Technology
New Delhi 110045

Printed at

Salasar Imaging Systems
Delhi 110035

To
My Parents

Contents

TABLES

ILLUSTRATIONS

(between pages 96–7)

1

Introduction

The Problem

A considerable volume of medieval Hindi literature consists of lengthy poetic compositions written in a genre variously referred to as Indo-Sufi *masnavī* or Hindi Sufi *premākhyān*. Literally, *prem* means 'love' and *ākhyān*, 'narrative'. This term is generally taken to mean 'romance' in the literary sense. The *masnavī* genre includes works of extraordinary quality and sophistication that have enjoyed considerable popularity with diverse segments of South Asian literary audiences. The *masnavī* has a long pedigree in India itself, from the fourteenth to the nineteenth centuries (see Table 1.1). The genre has antecedents outside India, most immediately in Persian literature,[1] but also in the literatures in Turkic languages.[2]

Although the Indo-Sufi *masnavī* is best known in India and in the West through one particular work, the magnificent *Padmāvat* (also known as *Padmāvatī* and *Padumāvatī*, 1540), of Malik Muhammad Jayasi (b. 1493), the genre has produced many other works of exceptional merit. One of them, Maulana Daud's *Cāndāyan* (1379), which appeared close to the beginning of the Indo-Sufi *masnavī* tradition, is the subject of this study.

Although providing a precise formal definition of the *masnavī* is a matter of some complexity, it can be said that, in the Indian tradition, the *masnavī* is a poetic genre comprised of long narrative poems with characteristic metrical structures, on any of several different themes, and capable of Sufi allegorical interpretation. In general terms, the *masnavī* is a kind of allegorical romance. It is most often a tale—frequently drawing upon a *melange* of Indic, Persian, and even Arabic sources—of love, quest, adventure, suffering, and eventual redemption on the part of a mystic hero. The allegorical dimension lies in the symbolic correspondence between the characters and episodes in the poem and Sufi beliefs and practices.

This study has several distinct aims. In a way, the easiest of these is to present an introduction and interpretation of an important work written at the very beginning of a literary tradition, which has not received its due in scholarship on medieval Hindi literature. Scholarship on *Cāndāyan*, though limited, has provided useful insights, but I wish to redress what I consider to be an inadequate appreciation in earlier scholarship, both on *Cāndāyan* in particular and on the Indo-Sufi *masnavī* in general, of the particularly Sufi components of the genre.

This is not an unimportant or trivial point. Because of a general syncretistic thread running through much of the north Indian *bhakti* literature,[3] a thread that has commonly been seen to incorporate Sufi elements as part of a north Indian culture of devotion, it has been possible to interpret the *masnavī* as just another species of (particularly *nirguṇa*) *bhakti* poetry.[4] The cost of this approach has been a failure to appreciate that although the Indo-Sufi *masnavī* became a fully 'Indianized' genre, it nevertheless maintained a Sufi identity and was capable of coherent and consistent allegorical interpretation. Without this Sufi content in the foreground, it was all too easy to convert the *masnavī* into the *premākhyān*, at the cost of distortion of overall context and content.

Although it is not my purpose to chronicle the entire history of the *masnavī* on South Asian soil, an outline is presented. I discuss in some detail structural and thematic aspects of the genre, taking up in passing different conceptualizations of precisely what it comprises. This is followed by an overview of the history of the genre, beginning with a discussion of the Persian *masnavī* and moving on to a brief history of its development in India. Chapter 1 concludes with a discussion of earlier literature on the Indo-Sufi *masnavī*, particularly as it applies to this study.

In Chapter 2, I turn my attention to Maulana Daud and his major work, *Cāndāyan*. I discuss the available historical sources that provide the basis for Daud's biography. This is followed by a description of the manuscript sources available for studying *Cāndāyan*. While it is not the aim here to compile a critical edition of *Cāndāyan*, it is absolutely essential to make clear the textual sources upon which my analysis rests, and I catalogue the manuscripts and published editions of *Cāndāyan* and relevent secondary literature. An outline of *Cāndāyan* follows and then the language of the text is discussed.

In Chapter 3 I turn my attention to the formal structure of *Cāndāyan*. This consists of an exposition of the characteristic format of the genre, leading to a discussion of the thematic features of the text. A discussion on the Indo-Sufi *masnavī's* metrical structure follows.

In Chapter 4, I present an extended exegesis of the Sufi content of *Cāndāyan*, showing thematic parallels drawn from Persian literature. In Chapter 5, I elaborate on my analysis by providing lengthy interpretations of two sections of the narrative, the snakebite episodes and the home-coming episode. In the concluding portion I return to the matter of whether *Cāndāyan* should best be considered a Sufi allegory or a devotional *Premākhyān*. Arguing for the former, I show that this is less terminological quibble, than a question central to the understanding of the entire work in its historical and cultural context.

Nature and Structure of the Indo-Sufi Masnavī

The *masnavī* as a literary genre enjoyed considerable popularity. Works in this genre vary to some degree in content, structure, and literary quality, and my attempt to characterize the genre as a whole may not do full justice to any particular *masnavī*. Nevertheless, it is worth our while to attempt to describe as clearly as possible the set of traits that define the *masnavī*, taking care to differentiate the *masnavī* from other poetic genres.

The *masnavīs* flourished in northern India and in southern outposts such as Golconda and Bijapur from the fourteenth to nineteenth centuries. In the northern tradition, works by a dozen or more major writers survive,[5] and there is a comparable number by poets of the Deccan.[6] The language of the northern recension of the *masnavī* is Awadhi,[7] while that of the southern tradition is Dakkani Hindi/Urdu.

Masnavī are long narrative poems (ranging from approximately 200 to more than 500 stanzas of variable length) on themes capable of having a Sufi allegorical interpretation. Plots of the Indo-Sufi *masnavīs* could be adapted from a wide variety of sources, including Islamic religion and mythology (e.g. *Yousuf-Zulaikhā* and *Lailā-Majnūn*), Persian folklore (e.g. *Sīrīn-Khusrau*), and Indian folklore and history (e.g. *Cāndāyan* and *Padmāvat*). The Arabic, Persian, and Indic strands are often interwoven into a pastiche of love, quest, adventure, suffering, and eventual redemption. There generally is a one-to-one correspondence between structural elements of the poem and the tenets of Sufi religious belief and practice.

In terms of form, the *masnavī* falls into a regular structure. Although on the surface the text of the *masnavī* continues stanza after stanza in an unbroken fashion without obvious divisions into larger segments, it actually can be said that the first part of any given Indo-Sufi *masnavī* comprises of the *stuti khaṇḍa* (literally, praise portion). The *stuti khaṇḍa* is that portion of the text dedicated to the praise of God, the Prophet, the reigning king, the patron, and the spiritual Shaikh, though not necessarily in that order. Different poets have allocated different numbers of stanzas to the *stuti khaṇḍa*, often followed by those stanzas wherein the author may present his justification for composing the *masnavī*. Generally, soon after the above formalities are completed, the main story of the *masnavī* begins.

A detailed description of the city or village of the hero or heroine sets up the background and atmosphere. This is followed by the circumstance which becomes instrumental in the first sighting or meeting of the hero and heroine. Sometimes this culminates in either falling in love and/or physical union. A period of separation ensues and the hero often leaves his village and the comforts of civilization to wander in the forest in quest of his beloved. The suffering of the hero and heroine is described in detail. If the hero is married, as the protagonist Lorik is in *Cāndāyan*, the suffering of his wife is also depicted. After practising austerities and suffering physically, the hero goes through a spiritual transformation. The story may have a happy ending (e.g. *Mṛgāvatī*), or end in a tragedy (e.g. *Padmāvat*).

It must be kept in mind that the above-mentioned components may be shuffled and need not follow each other in the order described above. The last part of the *masnavī* sometimes contains a stanza or two in which the author encapsulates the lesson he wishes to impart to his readers. In *Padmāvat*, Jayasi provides a key to the text so as to enable the reader to enjoy the story on the spiritual and secular levels. In *Mṛgāvatī*, the author sums up his *masnavī* with the instruction that one must continuously be engaged in the remembrance of God.

In terms of the meter, the Indo-Sufi *masnavīs* are composed in units that comprise a combination of *caupāī* and *dohā* verses. This poetic unit, called *kaḍvak*, is comparable to the stanza form. Composers of the Indo-Sufi *masnavīs* have experimented with different numbers of *caupāī* lines followed by a *dohā*. The *dohā* is a kind of couplet, each line having 24 morae that can be further divided in hemistitches of 13 and 11 morae.[8] An important feature of Indo-Sufi *masnavī* literature is that it is composed by combining two popular Indic poetic forms in a single unit. This unit does not follow the tenets of Persian prosody. However, poetic forms similar to that of the *kaḍvak* of the Indo-Sufi *masnavī* were in use in contemporary Persian literature. The prosody of the Indo-Sufi *masnavī* is discussed in Chapter 3 in some detail.

The Place of the Masnavī *in the History of Hindi Literature*

The appearance of Maulana Daud's *Cāndāyan* (completed in AD 1379), by common consensus, marks, the beginning of the era of Indo-Sufi *masnavī* literature in India. When Delhi became a centre of learning around the first quarter of the thirteenth century, litterateurs came to India from the northwest in quest of patronage. Scholars of Arabic, Persian, and Turkic brought with them literary forms that were new to India, such as the *ghazal*, *rubāī*, and *masnavī*, and these became popular. After some time, these litterateurs and their followers began to experiment with the local languages, dialects, and literary forms.

While retaining many of the structural features and thematic values of the original Persian form of the *masnavī, Cāndāyan* and the *masnavīs* that followed began to describe Indian landscapes, native rituals, and customs. Most of the *masnavīs* draw on Indic materials for inspiration. For example, the inspiration for *Cāndāyan* comes from a locally popular folktale, 'Cāndā and Lorik'. The story of *Padmāvat* is based on the siege of Chittor. An exclusive feature of Indic literature, *bārahmāsā*, which describes in detail seasonal changes throughout the year, was incorporated into the contents. As stated, most of the Indo-Sufi *masnavīs* are composed in Awadhi, the northernmost of the eastern Hindi vernaculars. These are written in Arabic script modified to accommodate the phonology of the Awadhi language.

As mentioned before, the *masnavī* genre has a long history in Persia and Turkey even before Daud composed his *Cāndāyan* in Awadhi. The literature that evolved from this synthesis is different both from Persian literature in Iran, on the one hand, and from other vernacular literature in South Asia. Daud's *Cāndāyan*, which marks the beginning of the Indo-Sufi tradition, is important not only because it is the first surviving Indian *masnavī*, but also because it marks the beginning of the indigenizing process. By virtue of having been the first *masnavī* in Hindi, *Cāndāyan* seems to have served as a model for Kutuban's *Mṛgāvatī* (1503), Jayasi's *Padmāvat* (1540), and Manjhan's *Madhumālatī* (1945). Most scholars agree that the chain of the Indo-Sufi *masnavī* genre which began with *Cāndāyan* continued until the beginning of the present century (Nasir's *Prem-darpan* 1917), sharing common formal properties and thematic contents.

Although *Cāndāyan* is perhaps not as well known as Jayasi's *Padmāvat*, it is nevertheless a work of comparable artistic merit and historical importance. Scholars such as Mataprasad Gupta, Shyam Manohar Pandey, Parashuram Chaturvedi, Shiv Kumar Shandilya, Peter Gaeffke, and Charlotte Vaudeville, have studied various aspects of the Indo-Sufi *masnavīs* composed in the north and south of India. Thus far, *Cāndāyan* is considered the earliest Indo-Sufi *masnavī* written in the Awadhi dialect. For this reason alone, it serves as an important landmark in the development of northern Indian vernacular literature.

The *masnavī* genre has a long history even before Daud. In simple terms, this narrative form involves a highly stylized and structured format using one of a small set of meters. Jalaluddin's thirteenth-century *Masnavī-i-Mānavī* is widely considered the exemplar of this genre in Persian.

With the establishment of Islamic courts in northern India, such important Persian literary genres as the *masnavī, ghazal*, and *rubāī* came onto Indian soil. Although poems in these genres were originally written in Persian, with the passage of time poets began to produce compositions in vernacular languages alongside their Persian prototypes. *Masnavīs* in Persian continued to be composed. For example, although four *masnavīs* had been composed in the Awadhi dialect in the course of the previous 200 years, Faizī, the court poet of Akbar (1542–1605), preferred to write his *masnavīs* in Persian. As early as the fourteenth and fifteenth centuries, these vernacular graftings took on a life of their own and served as the starting points for a Hindi-Sufi literary tradition. The form of language used for this literature was then known as Hinduī/Hindawi, with a core Indo-Aryan grammar enriched by many words borrowed from Arabic, Turkic, and Persian.

Scholars of Hindi literature who first studied *masnavī* in the early twentieth century, e.g. Ramchandra Shukla, Chandra Bali Pandey, and Parashuram Chaturvedi, appreciated the *masnavī* on a purely literary basis. They complained about the similarity of the plots without considering the allegorical nature of the genre. As a result, they missed the mystical content of these works. Mystical expression and interpretation is in fact the key element in this genre. In a *masnavī*, the spiritual aspect of the story is more important than its literary aspect. The sad part is that the next generation of scholars who were trained by this school of scholars accepted such an evaluation of the Indo-Sufi *masnavī* without question.[9] In this way, the Indo-Sufi *masnavī* literature, in general, remained in a state of neglect for several years.

In recent years, Hazariprasad Dwivedi, Shyam Manohar Pandey, Parmeshvarilal Gupta, Mataprasad Gupta, and Yash Gulati, among others, have worked hard to reintroduce the *masnavī* to readers. They have explored and interpreted the Sufi aspect and, to a certain degree, have been successful in restoring to this genre of literature the respect that is its due. Nevertheless, to date, the majority of the workon the Indo-Sufi *masnavī* genre is in Hindi, and the genre is largely unexplored by European scholars, with a few exceptions (e.g. Gaeffke and Vaudeville). *Cāndāyan* has not yet been, to my knowledge, translated into English. More importantly, it is the Sufi perspective which favours the mystical over the literary. The contribution of this volume is to help advance the knowledge and appreciation of a relatively under researched area of Hindi literature. Very little of this type of literature has been discussed, translated into European languages, or commented on by scholars with the exception of Aditya Behl and Simon Weightman's translation of Manjhan's *Madhumālatī*'.

Masnavī in the Persian Tradition

Let us briefly examine Persian *masnavī* literature in its historical context, and explore how it has been perceived. Defining the Persian *masnavī*, E.G. Browne writes,

> Concerning the many rhymed poem, or *mathnavi*, little need be said, since most European poetry which is not written in blank verse belongs to this category. The rhyme is contained in the *bayt*, (the unit in every species of poem, consists of two symmetrical halves), and changes from *bayt* to *bayt*. All long narrative and systematized didactic poems in Persian, like the *Shāhnāma*, or the Epic of Kings, of Firdawsī, the *Panj Ganj*, or Five Treasures, of Nizamī of Ganjā; the *Haft Awrang*, or Seven Thrones, of Jāmī; and the great Mystical *Mathnawī*, of Jalālud-Dīn-Rūmī, are composed in this form, which is of Persian invention, and unknown in classical Arabic poetry, though occasionally employed in post-classical Arabic verse by Persian writers. (Browne 1928: 26)

Introducing the rhyme scheme and the prosody of the *masnavi*, George Morrison writes:

> The *masnavī* is a long poem in rhyming hemistichs. It is an Iranian form; the *Yashts* or hymns of the Avesta are somewhat similar in form, consisting of metrical lines, not however rhyming. As early as Rudakī we have traces of *masnavī* poems. Firdausī used this form for the *Shahnameh*. Fragments of two *masnavīs* of Unsurī survive. Asadī wrote the epic *Garshāspnāmeh* as a *masnavī*. The romantic *masnavī*, *Varqeh o Gulshāh*, of Ayyuqi was followed by the *Vīs o Rāmīn* of Fakhr ad-Din Asad Gurgānī in the middle of the eleventh century. This in turn served as the inspiration for the romantic *masnavīs* of Nizamī of Ganjeh. . . . Perhaps the most famous of all are the *Masnavī* of Jalālud-Dīn Rūmī,

a poem on a huge scale traditionally called the Qur'ān in Persian, and the long *Shāhnāmeh*, the epic poem begun by Daqiqi and finished as the work of a lifetime by Firdausī, 936–1020. (Morrison 1981: 10)

Muhammad Sadiq's definition of the Indian *masnavī* is very similar to Browne's:

A *masnavī* is the name given to a poem written in rhyming couplets. It is the most suitable form for descriptive and narrative verse, as well as for didactic, mystical or ethical themes. All long poems, like the *Śāhnāmā* of Firdausī and the *Masnavī* of Jalaluddin Rumi are composed in this form. The genre was not known to the Arabs, and was developed by the Persians out of the *rajāz* couplet which the Arabs scarcely consented to dignify with the name of poetry. (Sadiq 1964: 39)[10]

From the above definitions, two points are clear. First, *masnavī* is the name given to a meter generally known as rhymed verse. Second, the *masnavī* is also the name of a literary genre in which a long allegorical, didactic, narrative poem is composed in a designated meter. As a literary genre, the *masnavī* prospered and flourished, rapidly achieving great heights of artistic beauty and popularity in the Persian and Turkic languages.

Etymologically, the term *masnavī* has evolved from the Arabic root *se-alif-nūn*. The noun derived from this root is *sānī*, literally 'double' (cf. Hebrew *miśna*).

As mentioned before, the *masnavī* as a literary genre prospered and flourished in the Persian and Turkic languages. Throughout the world, the very word *masnavī* has come to mean *The Masnavī* of Jalaluddin Rumi (d. 1273), said to be revered by Sufis as the Koran. It is perhaps the most discussed Persian work. Many commentaries have been written on its literal meaning and mystical interpretations.

Reynold A. Nicholson has discussed the thematic content of Rumi's *Masnavī* and its parent genre (i.e. the *qasīda*). He explains why the *masnavī* does not find endorsement and legitimacy in Arabic literature but enjoys a high place in the Persian literary world. He then proceeds to discuss the mystic nature of the *masnavī*. He writes:

One of the deepest differences between Arabs and Persians shows itself in the extent and character of the mystical poetry of each people. As regards Persia, the names of Sana'i, 'Attar, Jalalu'ddin Rumi, S'adi, Hafiz, and J'ami are witnesses enough. Whether quantity or quality be considered, the best part of medieval Persian poetry is either genuinely mystical in spirit or is so saturated with mystical ideas that it will never be more than half understood by those who read it literally.

His analysis continues:

> When we turn to Arabic poetry of the period subsequent to the rise and development of Sufism, what do we find? No lack of poets, certainly, though few of them reach the first rank and their output is scanty compared with the opulent genius of their Persian contemporaries. But from Mutanabbi and Ma'arri down to the bards unknown in Europe who flourished long after the Baghdad Caliphate had fallen, it is remarkable how seldom they possess the note of mysticism. The main reason, I think, lies in racial endowment. The Arab has no such passion for an ultimate principle of unity as has always distinguished the Persians and Indians. He shares with other Semitic peoples an incapacity for harmonizing and unifying the particular facts of experience; he discerns the trees very clearly, but not the wood. Like his art, in which we everywhere find a delicate sense for detail, but nowhere large apprehension of a great and united whole. His poetry, intensely subjective in feeling and therefore lyrical in form, presents only a series of brilliant expressions full of life and colour, yet essentially fragments and moments of life, not fused into the substance of universal thought by an imagination soaring above place and time. (Nicholson 1977: xvi)

Modern scholars may not completely agree with Nicholson's views and even find his arguments offensive. However, for a long time he remained the major scholar of Persian literature. He was one of the first to open the *Masnavī* of Rumi to the West with a translation and commentary in four volumes.

Daud's *Cāndāyan* was completed approximately a hundred years after the *Masnavī* of Rumi. Therefore, what Nicholson has to say about the *masnavī* is of interest. According to Nicholson, the reason the Arabs favoured the *qasīdā*, while the Iranians and Indians embraced the *masnavī*, is embedded in the difference between Arab and Persian culture and philosophy. Nicholson gives the credit for the legitimacy of *qasīdā* in Arabic poetry to the limitations of a nomadic culture. The thematic content and poetic form are only reflections of the mode of life of the Arabs. According to him the *qasīdā* is suitable for elucidating the constantly shifting habitations of the wandering tribesmen seeking pasture throughout the winter and spring seasons. The poet must tell of his emotions, such as love, and he may describe the beauty of his beloved and tell of the terrain he passes through in the course of his migratory life, but all this has to be accomplished in a relatively short span of time. *Qasīdā*, by virtue of its relatively shorter and compartmentalized form, provides the framework for such expression.

On the other hand, according to Nicholson, although the outward lives of mystics are rarely eventful, the inner journey covers a broad vista of mystical experiences. The relatively unrestricted framework and the unlimited scope of subject matter make the *masnavī* not just attractive but the ideal vehicle to express the mystic discourse.[11]

In terms of history, these were the times when, because of the political and territorial ambitions of the reigning monarchs of India and her northwesterly neighbours, frontiers of the northwest were costantly in a state of flux. With the beginning of the Mongol onslaught on western Asia, several intellectuals sought shelter in places like Bhakkar at the court of Nasiruddin Qabaca, at Multan and at Ucch. Many of these immigrants later moved to Delhi with Iltutmish.

Political instability contributed greatly to the migration of many scholars, artists, and noblemen from Central Asia and Persia to the Indian peninsula. *Tārīkh-i-Jahān-gushā*, the *Jāmī'ut-Tawārīkh*, and the works of Sir Henry Howorth describe the sufferings endured by Persia and Asia Minor as well as Central Asia and China at the hands of the Mongol rulers Chingīz Khān (1219–27) and Halāqū Khān (1255–65). In Browne's words:

> The several periods of Mongol ascendancy in Persia may be said to extend from the first invasion of that country by Chingīz Khān in AD 1219 to the death of Abu Sa'īd Khān in AD 1335 to which succeeded half a century of anarchy, culminating in another Tartar invasion, that of Tīmūr-i-Lang better known in Europe as Tamerlane. (Browne 1926: 443)

Development of *Masnavī* on the Indian Subcontinent

The early *masnavīs*, such as the *Khamsā*, a collection of five *masnavīs* dedicated to Alauddin Khilji, and the *Nuh Sipahr* (*Nine Spheres*) of Amir Khusrau (d. 1325), were composed in India in the Persian language and Arabic script. In India during the early centuries of the second millennium, in addition to Amir Khusrau, many great authors were writing in Persian. Cataloguing these early compositions, Schimmel writes:

> Khusrau, though he is considered the outstanding medieval Indo-Persian poet and at the same time the inaugurator of Hindustani music, was by no means the first great poet in the subcontinent to write in Persian; rather he perfected a tradition that had been alive for more than two centuries. In addition to the historical works such as *Tabaqāt-i-Nasiri* of Menhaj al Siraj (d. 1260), the great Sufi mystic Hujviri, also known as Datā Ganj Bakhsh (d. 1071), wrote his *Kāśaf al-mahjūb* in the Persian language in Lahore. This book is a treatise on early mystical ideas and practices. Abu al Faraj Runi (d. 1091) was a master of the *qasīdā* form of poetry, Masaud Sad-e Salman (d. 1131) wrote his *habsiyyāt*

(prison poems) and poems of the *shahr-āshub* in Persian. (Schimmel 1988, also see M Mujeeb 1985: 282–336)

Although it is true that authors in India were writing in Persian before him, Khusrau was the first to compose poems in Persian and Hindawi simultaneously. They were later used in *qawwali*. His *masnavīs* are composed in Persian and some of the *qawwali, murkis*, and riddles are in Hindawi, later classified as Awadhi, the easternmost dialect of the Hindi language.

Amir Khusrau was a leading and well-respected author and statesman even in his own time. His writings endorse and even extol the virtues of India, and have contributed a great deal toward the evolution of the Indo-Sufi *masnavī* by endowing it with respectability and legitimacy. In fact, Amir Khusrau wrote a number of poems in which the first line of a couplet is in Persian and the rhyming second line is in Hindawi. One of these poems has survived and has become very popular in *qawwali* form. This composition is a good example of the process of indigenization and appropriation. The first hemistitch of the opening couplet is in the Persian language followed by the second hemistitch in Hindawi.

> *Ze hāl-i-miskīn, ma kun taghāful,*
> Do not ignore the condition of the distraught (lover).
>
> *Dorāye nainā, banāye batiyān.*
> She turns her glances away and spins a long tale.

The third hemistich again is in Persian, followed by a fourth in Hindawi:

> *Keh tāb-i-hijrān, nadāram ei jān*
> Darling, I have no stamina for the pain of separation.
>
> *Na leho kāhe lagāya chatiyān!* (Zaidi 1993: 24)
> Why don't you just give me a hug!

In addition to the above, Amir Khusrau composed riddles and couplets explaining the meaning of certain lexical items from the Turkic, Persian, Hindawi, and Arabic registers. These couplets are composed in a mixture of Persian, Arabic, Turkic, and Hindawi and, luckily, some have survived. Here is an example:[12]

> *Wālid, bāp, beṭā farzand*
> *Dukhtar beṭī, sīkh hai pand.* (Tiwari 1985: 145)

The Arabic word *wālid* is a synonym of *bāp* meaning father; *beṭā* (son) is the Hindi equivalent of Persian *farzand*. Dukhtar in Persian is *beṭī* in Hindi; and the Hindi word *sīkh* is *pand* in Persian, meaning sermon.

Although over time the language of the Indo-Sufi *masnavī* changed from Persian to Awadhi, the script by and large remained Persian, except in the case of the author Nur Muhammad (Jindal 1993: 44).

Having mentioned Amir Khusrau's compositions in different languages and his love for India, I should add that *masnavīs* were continuously composed in India in the Persian language for approximately 250 years before *Cāndāyan* was written in Awadhi. It is only natural that the early immigrant scholars were writing in Persian, the language they knew best, and in the literary genres they were familiar with, such as the *masnavī*, the *ghazal*, and the *qasīdā*. They looked to Persian models for inspiration, thematic content and imagery. Nevertheless, in time, their descriptions began to appear artificial and the imagery seemed entirely imported. For example, here are a few lines from one of Amir Khusrau's *masnavī*, *Duwal Rani Khazir Khan*:

Parastārān-i-ū nīz-i-andar īn gham
Cū margh-e-gandah pur oftādeh purkam
Neśasteh narges-i-paz murdeh bīmar
Beh makhmūrī-o-safrā zard rukhsār (Nizami: 1988: 116).

In this sorrow, those who are devoted to her
Resemble a bird whose feather has been plucked
Like withered wilted flowers of narcissus
Faint, pale cheeked, as if about to pass out.

Comparison of half-open eyes with the wilted narcissus and imagery of the sick bird that had shed its feathers, although common in the Persian poetic tradition, gradually became unfamiliar to the Indians. This obviously left a vacuum creating an opening for change in the *masnavī* genre. Muhammad Mujeeb traces some of the steps early writers, who did most of their work in Persian, took toward assimilating Indian elements into the *masnavī* genre.

In one of his historical *masnavīs*, the *Nuh Siphr*, or the Nine Skies, written to celebrate the glories of the reign of Qutubuddin Mubarak, Amir Khusrau has devoted a whole section, the Third Sky, to the description and praise of India and the Indians. He likens India to Paradise and shows that because of its fruits, flowers and climate, it is better than any other country. The Indians excel in science and wisdom; they are the inventors of numerals, the creators of the *Panchatantra*, the great book of worldly wisdom which has been translated into Persian, Turkish, Arabic and Dari; their music surpasses the music of any other country. (Mujeeb 1985: 173–4).

The process of assimilation, improvization, and embellishment in the indigenous language began with the composition of *Cāndāyan*. Many of the structural features and thematic values of the original form of the *masnavī* are retained in *Cāndāyan*, but the description of the landscape, flora and fauna, and rituals and customs are essentially Indian. For inspiration *Cāndāyan* draws on a popular local folktale, 'Cāndā and Lorik'. Composed in Awadhi, it incorporates literary conventions like the *bārahmāsā*, exclusive to Indian literature. A *bārahmāsā* describes the seasonal changes over the year and the corresponding changes in a heroine's moods. The literature that emerged from the synthesis of the Persian *masnavī* tradition and Indic literary traditions is unique. The many *masnavīs* composed in this genre are classified under the rubric Indo-Sufi *masnavī* literature, or, in the historical context of Hindi literature, the rubric *Premākhyān*.

As the years passed, poets composing *masnavīs* in India began to replace descriptions of the Persian landscape with Indian scenery. They also adopted Indic literary features. As a result of this transformation the Persian *masnavī* evolved into the Indo-Islamic *masnavī*.

Although the Indian Sufi poets retained many of the structural and thematic features of the original *masnavī* genre, they began to describe Indian birds, flowers, markets, villages, historical events, and battles. Moreover, rituals and customs of the Hindu scene began to be reflected. For example, in *kaḍvak 279* of *Cāndāyan* (M. Gupta 1967), after consulting the astrologer about the configuration of the planets, the hero Lorik decides to cross the Ganga and move east after eloping with the heroine. Similarly, in *kaḍvak* 64, the ritual of applying vermilion on the forehead and in the part of a married woman's hair is described. In short, soon after the *masnavīs* of Amir Khusrau were composed, the indigenization process became more and more manifest in *masnavīs* such as *Mṛgāvatī* and *Padmāvat* (1503, 1540, respectively).

Awadhi was known at the time as Hindawi or Hindui. (The Hindi language, as we know it today, had not yet evolved.) Awadhi grammar is Indo-Aryan but in *Cāndāyan*, the earliest available *masnavī*, many words are incorporated from Arabic, Turkic, and Persian. In fact, in *Cāndāyan*, the introduction to each of the episodes is in Persian prose. Interestingly, Malik Muhammad Jayasi's *Padmāvat*, composed approximately a 100 years later, seems to have a considerably smaller number of Arabic and Persian words.[13]

After their emigration to India, Sufi mystics undertook a study of Indian languages and philosophical systems. A few of them learned Sanskrit and translated its literature and poetic treatises into Persian. Settling into their new environment, they also learned the vernacular languages. The consequence was a borrowing of the local languages and cultural features. In other words, local folklore and regionally popular customs came to be portrayed in the Indo-Sufi *masnavīs* with increasing frequency.

A number of authors of the early *masnavīs*, in particular, were either well-known Sufi figures or were affiliated with a major order of the Sufis. Therefore *masnavī* literature is generally catalogued as the Indo-Sufi *masnavī*, as opposed to other love narratives composed at the same time. For example, Maulana Daud, the author of *Cāndāyan*, was a disciple of the nephew of the Sufi Shaikh Nasiruddin Chiragh-i-Delhi, who, in turn, was a disciple of Hazrat Nizamuddin Aulia of Delhi (d. 1325), perhaps the most famous shaikh of the Chishti Sufi order in India.[14]

Similarly, *Mṛgāvatī* was written by Kutuban, who lived in Jaunpore and was the disciple of Sheikh Burhan. Malik Muhammad, who lived in Jayasi and composed *Padmāvat*, was a disciple of Shaikh Muhiuddin, who, in turn had been a disciple of Shaikh Burhan. Jayasi stands ninth in the hierarchy of Chishti saints (Jindal 1993: 39).

Most of the Indo-Sufi *masnavīs* were composed by Sufis. Often the concluding *kaḍvak* of the *masnavīs* offers a table of the characters and/or events of the story and how it should be interpreted from the Sufi perspective. For instance, in the concluding chapter of his *Padmāvat*, to clarify his Sufi message, Malik Muhammad Jayasi explains that *chittore* stands for the body, the king symbolizes of the mind, *sinhala* signifies the heart, and the parrot represents the teacher who shows the king the path to Padminī, the ultimate intelligence (Gulati 1979: 142).[15]

Commenting on the mystical interpretation of the *masnavī*, Jindal writes:

> The Sufis never described a story for the sake of the story. The purpose is to depict the love of the soul for God and its ultimate union with Him. The story of two human lovers is only an allegory. Jayasi himself explains to us at the end of his book how the different characters can be allegorically interpreted. Jayasi and his predecessors have made their heroes suffer a lot, often turning out to be mendicants, for the sake of their beloved—how else could they have symbolized the difficulties in the path of self-purification and the possibilities of ultimate realization. (Jindal 1993: 41)?

The *Masnavī* in the Context of the History of Hindi Literature

Although it is possible, and even desirable, to view the Indo-Sufi *masnavī* as a part of a chain having connections back to Persian literature in its Iranian homeland, it is also important to realize that this genre has been assigned a place in the development of Hindi literature. There are numerous possible periodizations to be sure; nevertheless there are some features that are common to the most important among them. In general, the flow of Hindi literature is divided into a number of eras (or *kāls*) extending from an era of bardic chronicles (*Vīr gāthā kāl* or *Ādi kāl*) to the modern period (*Ādhunik kāl*).

The age of the Indo-Sufi and non-Sufi love narratives, *Madhya yugīn premākhyān*, according to R.L. Handa and H. Mishra, lies between the age of the bardic chronicles, *Vīr gāthā kāl* or *Ādi kāl* (908–1300), and the middle part of the age of the devotional literature, *Bhakti kāl* (1300–1600). Scholars such as Shukla, Chaturvedi, and Dwivedi have arranged Hindi literature in four general chronological categories: (1) the early period, *Ādi kāl* (tenth to fourteenth centuries); (2) the age of devotional poetry, *Bhakti kāl* (fourteenth to sixteenth centuries); (3) the age of classicism, *Rīti kāl* (sixteenth to nineteenth centuries); and (4) the age of modern consciousness, *Ādhunik kāl* (mid-nineteenth century to the present). This classification and various sub-classifications are widely accepted by Jindal, Mishra, and Shivalochana Pandey (Mishra 1967: 10). A brief description of the periods and their literature follow.

The period when the earliest recorded lyrical poetry was composed in the contemporary dialects of Hindi is called the *Ādi kāl*. The highlight of this period is a body of bardic chronicles composed in the *Dingal* dialect by bards employed by Rajputs (for example, *Khummaṇ Rāso, Baladev Rāso, Pṛthvīrāj Rāso, Hammīr Riāso*, and *Dholā Mārū*). The bravery, nobility, achievements, and praise of the Rajput are the dominant themes. However, the poems of the Nath Yogis and the Siddhas, as well as the poetry of early Sufis such as Baba Farid (1173–1267), Hamiduddin Nagauri (1182–1274), and Bū Ali Qaladar (d. 1323), are also part of the literature belonging to the *Ādi kāl* (Jindal 1993: 38–9).

Some issues about the literature belonging to the *Ādi kāl* are worth noting at this point. Perhaps by virtue of their lyrical quality, the poems of the early Sufis of India, composed in Hindawi, the eastern dialect of Hindi, are placed together with the poetry of *Ādi kāl*, even though the two genres are quite different in essence. In contrast, the Indo-Sufi *masnavī* literature, which is narrative in nature, is put in a separate category along with a number of long narrative poems not written by Sufis. The era of the Hindi *premākhyān* is that of most of the long narrative poems and includes, as well, the Indo-Sufi *masnavīs*. The Hindi *premākhyān* and the Indo-Sufi *masnavī* together constitute the literature of the *Bhakti kāl*, the next chronological age. According to Jindal, the Sufis authors must have perceived it necessary to demonstrate their familiarity with the Hindawi language. He quotes Saiyid Athar Abbas: 'Persian-speakers had to use Hindawi to establish their contact with the local population. At Sufi hermitages, particularly Baba Farid's (1174–1265) one could not do without Hindawi. At Sheikh Hamid ud-Din Nagauri's home (d. 1274), Hindawi was much in use' (Jindal 1993: 13).

In support of the above, in a discussion of the interaction between medieval Hindu mystic traditions and Sufism, Saiyid Athar Abbas Rizvi writes:

> From the eleventh century onwards in India, the contacts and conflicts between sufis and yogis became more frequent and meaningful. The various branches of qalandars and sufis of the Rafaiya order, confined mainly to Turkey, Syria and Egypt, were significantly influenced by wandering yogis. Unfortunately existing literature throws little light on yogis, who are constantly referred to as jogis. In one reference the perfect yogi is associated by Shaikh Nasirud Din Chiragh-i-Delhi with the Siddhas. The topics discussed at the jamā at-k͟hāna gatherings of Baba Farid were of great interest to visiting Siddhas whose beliefs were founded on Hath Yoga. (Rizvi 1975: 323–96)

Rizvi describes in some detail the exchanges which regularly occurred between sufis and yogis on their beliefs and practices. In the Sufi writings, this new knowledge found ample expression, giving rise to a remarkable literary synthesis.

Bhakti kāl, the age of devotional literature, followed *Ādi kāl*. *Bhakti kāl* is generally divided into two parts. The early part of the *Bhakti kāl* is also known as the period of transition (R.P. Mishra 1982: 13) or the *Madhya yug* (S.M. Pandey 1982). Indo-Sufi *masnavī* literature, because of its narrative character and mystical nature, is placed in the first half of the age of devotional literature. The second half is constituted by the work of such famous poets as Kabīr, Sūr, Mīrā, Raidās, Rāmdās, and Tulasidās, belonging variously to the *nirguṇ* (devoid of physical attributes) and *saguṇ* (having attributes) branches of devotional poetry.

The age of the *Bhakti* yielded to the age of classicism, *Rīti kāl*. Many of the famous Sanskrit classics were translated or rewritten in dialects of Hindi. Gokulnāth, Dwārkā Prasād Mishra, Manideva, Kṛṣṇadās,

Giridhar, among others, were outstanding contributors to the *Rīti kāl* (R.P. Mishra 1982: 77–98).

Rīti kāl was succeeded by the period of modern Hindi literature, *Ādhunik kāl*, which again is divided into subclassifications according to literary trends and influences. In addition, *Ādhunik kāl* includes the prose literature of modern *kharī bolī* Hindi.

The focus of this study is the Indo-Sufi *masnavī* literature that was first composed during what Jindal calls the age of the Sufi Cult, fourteenth to the nineteenth centuries (Jindal 1993: 36). According to Jindal, there was no consensus among early scholars of the history of Hindi literature about the chronological placement of the Indo-Sufi *masnavī* genre. Handa discusses literature composed by the Sufis after Sant Kabīr (1398–1518) and Guru Nanak (b. 1469) (Handa 1978: 121–32). Ramchandra Shukla is also confused about the position of the Indo-Sufi *masnavīs*[16] and begins his discussion of the Indo-Sufi *masnavī* genre with Jayasi. He declares that the *Bhakti kāl* ended in 1700. However, in a later edition of the same book, he discusses *Indrāvatī*, a *masnavī* composed by Nur Muhammad, completed in 1801 but placed by error in the so-called *Bhakti kāl* (Singh 1989: 39–40). Similarly, according to Rastogi and Sharan, the era of the Indo-Sufi *masnavī* genre begins with Jayasi's *Padmāvat*, completed in 1540, and ends with Fazil Shah's *Prem Ratan*, completed in 1905 (Rastogi 1988: 230–9).

From the above observations there seems to be general agreement that the period when the Indo-Sufi *masnavīs* were composed closely follows the *Ādi kāl* and blends with the period when the *nirguṇ* and *saguṇ bhakti* movements were in full bloom (1450 to 1550). Modern scholarship has brought to light the fact that the first Indo-Sufi *masnavī* was composed in 1379, much earlier than previously thought. Additionally, we now know that the composition of Indo-Sufi *masnavīs* continued for a much longer time (in both north India and in the south) than that given by early scholars. This discovery has increased the volume of Indo-Sufi *masnavī* literature considerably and warrants a closer look. Based on geographical location and linguistic characteristics, modern scholars now divide Indo-Sufi *masnavī* poetry into a northern and a southern branch (Jindal 1993: 43).

Chronology of Indo-Sufi *Masnavī* Compositions

Indo-Sufi *masnavī* literature spans over 500 years. According to Shukla, (Daud's *Cāndāyan*) to 1917 (Nasir's *masnavī* entitled *Prem-Darpan*).

Referring to the southern branch of the Indo-Sufi *masnavī* literature, i.e. the *masnavī* literature composed in the southern princely states and kingdoms of India, Pathak writes, 'Similar to the Hindi romances of north India, the Hindi romances of south India have their specific tradition' (Pathak 1978: 252). Jindal elaborates on this theme:

> One of the significant distinguishing differences between the Indo-Sufi *masnavī* of north India and south India was the use of the language. Among the Sufis of the Deccan, Mirājī Shams-ul Ushshāq (1496–1562), Burhanuddin Janam (1543–98) and Shāh Amin (1598–1675)—father, son, and grandson—seem to be the most distinguished. When we look at their vocabulary, it becomes evident that they have freely used Marathi and Sanskrit words without any inhibition—in the same way that they have used the esoteric metaphysical terminology of Vedanta and Yoga—which again is all Sanskrit, *tatsama* or *tadbhava*. (Jindal 1993: 43)

The stream of successive compositions by Daud, Kutuban, Jayasi and Manjhan had a pervasive influence on Deccan literature. It is wrong to think that the tradition of the north Indian literary romance vanished after having flourished for such a short time. In fact, from *Cāndāyan* (1379) to *Prem Darpan* (1917), the literary tradition of the Hindi *prem-ākhyān* continued in an unbroken sequence. According to Pathak, this tradition was established in the Deccan in 1404 in the Bahmani kingdom (Pathak 1978: 177).

Table 1.1 furnishes the names of some of the more important authors of the Indo-Sufi *masnavīs* available so far, the titles of their compositions, and the dates of their compositions:

Table 1.1. Indo-Sufi *Masnavīs* in Chronological Order

Name of the Author	Name of the *Masnavī*	Date
Mulla Daud	*Cāndāyan*	1379
Shaikh Kutuban	*Mṛgāvatī*	1503
Malik Muhammad Jayasi	*Padmāvat*	1540
Manjhan	*Madhumālatī*	1545
Shaikh Usman	*Citrāvalī*	1613
Kavi Jan	(12+ *masnavīs*)	
Shaikh Nabi	*Gyāndīp*	1618
Hussain Ali	*Puhupāvatī*	1725
Qasim Shah	*Haṁsa-jawāhar*	1736
Shaikh Nisar	*Yūsuf Zulaikhā*	1790
Shah Najaf Ali Saloni	*Akharāvatī*	1809
Khwaja Ahmad	*Nūrjahān*	1905
Nasir	*Prem Darpan*	1917

Scholarship on the Indo-Sufi Masnavī

Because significant numbers of South Asian *masnavī* manuscripts were not published until well into the twentieth century, the genre as a whole has not been as extensively described as others. Even within the genre, only Jayasi's *Padmāvat*, the first published Indo-Sufi *masnavī*, was commented on by Grierson, Shukla, and H. Dwivedi.[17]

Grierson's scholarship on this can be traced back to a published edition of *Padmāvat* brought out by the Asiatic Society of Bengal in 1897-1911. This was in turn followed by the publication by the Nāgarīpracāriṇī Sabhā of the so-called printed 'Benaras' edition of the text. In 1949, Lakshmi Dhar published a detailed study of the work that included a grammatical study and a comparative and etymological glossary of the *Padmāvat* text. Dhar's work was based on the following unpublished materials from the India Office Library catalogues and the Benaras edition of *Padmāvat* of the Nāgarīpracāriṇī Sabhā in 1924.

1. No. P. 1018 (PA). A folio written in Nastalīq characters with coloured illustrations. *Dohās* are in red ink. The name of the scribe is written above the colophon in ink.
2. No. P. 1975 (PB). This colophon was used as the base because the Nastalīq employs correct vowel markings. *Dohās* and the border are again in red.
3. No. P. 1819 (PC). In this manuscript, also written in Persian Nastalīq, Jayasi's *Bhajans* precede the actual text of the *Padmāvat*.
4. No. P. 3130 (PD). This manuscript has pages missing from the beginning and end of the text, subsequently supplied, by another scribe in Nastalīq, without enumeration of verses.
5. No. 2459 (PE). This copy is also in Nastalīq but is not well executed. *Dohās* are in red. There are many corrections in the margins.
6. No. S. 2471 (NM). This manuscript is in Nāgarī script. It is well written. The *Dohās* are in red ink, and most importantly, each *Caupāī* has a separate heading in red. (Many of the manuscripts of *Cāndāyan*, composed approximately 150 years earlier, also have a separate heading in Persian prose, written in red, before each *kaḍvak*.)
7. Benaras Edition (1924) by Nāgarīpracāriṇī Sabhā.[18]

In 1962, Bankey Behari's *Sufis, Mystics, and Yogis of India* was published. It sheds light on basic Sufi tenets such as the *tauhīd* (unity-consciousness), the seven stages in a Sufi's itinerary, aspects of conservative Sufism, and its subsequent transformation into pantheism.

From the point of view of interpretation on the mystic level, this work is important. The book is divided into two parts. Up to page 272, it is in English. The latter half is in the Devanagari script. This second section, in Devanagari script, opens with excerpts from the works of Persian mystics such as Sultan Abu Said. Verses are also taken from the sixth book of Rumi's *Masnavī*. Poetry composed in the Persian language is presented in the Devanagari script. Punjabi couplets of Baba Farid and Bullah Shah are also printed out in the Devanagari script. The work concludes with select verses of Kabir and Namdev.

Mataprasad Gupta's critical edition of *Padmāvat* was published in 1963. Its importance lies in the fact that this is perhaps the first time that serious questions were raised regarding Ramchandra Shukla's interpretation of the Indo-Sufi *masnavī* literature. Gupta says that, according to Shukla, the hero Ratnasen pursues Padmāvatī merely for her physical attributes, which is not true love, merely infatuation. 'The question is, should we accept Shukla's opinion as valid or is it possible to contemplate and examine this literature to find another solution/ interpretation' (M. Gupta 1963: 44)? Gupta's *Madhumālatī* was published in 1961 and *Mṛgāvatī* came out in 1968.

Sūfī Kāvya Saṁgrah of Parashuram Chaturvedi, published in 1965, begins by emphasizing that the Sufi poet's contribution to Hindi literature cannot be underestimated. Chaturvedi throws light on the concepts and practices of the Sufis. He discusses the contribution of the early Sufis, such as Bayazid, Junaid, Shubli, and Mansur, and proceeds to discuss Sufism, Indo-Sufi literature, and their symbolic interpretation. Most importantly, he gives a brief description of the *masnavī* from Daud's *Cāndāyan* to Nasir's *Prem-Darpan*. The concluding chapters present excerpts from the compositions of some of the most famous among the Indo-Sufi poets.

Chandra Bali Pandey's *Tasawwuf athavā Sūfimat* came out in 1966. In the first few pages, his book traces the beginnings of Sufism and discusses the beliefs of the Sufis, the symbols they used, and their philosophy. Pandey discusses Arabic and Persian literature and elaborates on the characteristics of Sufi verse and its subsequent influence on Indian vernacular literature (Pandey 1966: 156–71).

Sudha Saksena's *Jayasi ki Bimba Yojana* also came out in 1966. Saksena offers a detailed discussion of the intellectual, emotional, and imaginative elements in Jayasi's *Padmāvat*.

Ram Awadh Dwivedi's *A Critical Survey of Hindi Literature*, published in 1966, has a chapter entitled 'The Poetry of the Mystics: Jayasi, Usman,

Sheikh Nabi, and Noor Muhammad'. The highlight of this work is a discussion of Sufi philosophy with *Padmāvat* as its focus.

Shyam Manohar Pandey, the leading authority on *Cāndāyan* today, published his *Sūfī Kāvya Vimarśa* in 1968. It is a collection of several papers on different aspects of the poetry of Daud, Jayasi, and Manjhan.

Shrinivas Batra's *Hindī aur Fārasī Sūfī Kāvya kā Tulanātmak Adhyayan* was published in 1973. In my opinion, it is one of the most comprehensive studies on the subject of the Indo-Sufi *masnavī* genre. Not all scholars agree with Batra, who aims at a comparative study of Persian and Indo-Sufi *masnavī* literature. Nonetheless, one has to appreciate his work for its organization of a great deal of material and the breadth of its coverage.

Sarojini Pandey's *Hindī Sūfī Kāvya meṁ Pratīk Yojanā* (1974) discusses symbolism in Vedic, Classical Sanskrit, Prākṛt, and Apabhraṁśa poetry of the Siddhas with its subsequent appropriation and adaptation in Indo-Sufi *masnavī* literature.

Rajnath Sharma's *Jāyasī Granthāvalī* (1975) offers the reader a complete text of *Padmāvat*, including a glossary and commentary. The author claims that his aim is to present a clean and modern version of *Padmāvat*. Therefore, unlike Mataprasad Gupta's edition, Sharma's book opens with the text itself. It does not include any discussion of earlier works that may have had an influence on the composition of *Padmāvat*, the language of the *masnavī* or the historical incidents upon which the text was based.

Umapati Chandel's *Hindī Sūfī Kāvya me Paurāṇik Ākhyān* (1976) traces specific elements of stories from the Purāṇas that find mention in the Indo-Sufi *masnavīs*. A good example of this is the *Masnavī Nal-Daman*, which is based on the *Nalopākhyān* of the *Mahābhārata*.

Shivsahay Pathak's *Hindi Sufi Kāvya kā Samagra Anuśīlan* (1978) opens with a discussion of the beginning of Sufism, Sufism in India, and the significance of the Sufi *premākhyāns*. It culminates in a discussion of the spiritual aspects of the Indo-Sufi *masnavīs*. According to S.M. Pandey (1982–8), Pathak borrows from authors such as Pathak himself, S. Shukla, and R. Tiwari without citation.

The same year also brought Vidyadhar Tripathi's *Jāyasī ke Sāhitya meṁ Aprastut Yojanā* to the public. The main focus of this work is an analysis of the figures of speech in Jayasi's *Padmāvat, Akhrāvat, Ākhirī Kalām* and *Kaharnāma*, with particular emphasis on the use of metaphors.

Sūfī Kavitā kī Pahcān of Yash Gulati (1979) contains eight essays on the importance, symbolism, and philosophy of Indo-Sufi *masnavīs* such as *Padmāvat, Madhumālatī*, and *Kunvarāvat*.

Shyam Manohar Pandey's *Madhya Yugīna Premākhyāna* (1982) opens with a discussion of Sufi and Persian romance literature. It proceeds to discuss the stories about Duṣyanta and Śakuntalā, Nala and Damayantī, and Uṣā-Aniruddha, which occur in the religious texts of India. Pandey also touches on the Prākṛt romances such as the *Ṇāyakumāra Cariu* and moves on to romances in the vernacular languages. He makes a distinction between the romance literature with mystical elements (i.e. the Sufi romance) as opposed to narratives that are not mystical in nature. A comparative study of Sufi and non-Sufi romances follows. To this end, his work briefly discusses the symbolism in the romances composed in the north Indian vernaculars.

Chandra Sansar (1986), in *Some Prominent Muslim-Hindi Poets*, which introduces such poets and their works as Amir Khusrau (d. 1325), Daud, Kabīr, Kutuban, Abdul Quddus Gangohi, Jayasi, Manjhan, Usman, and Jankavi. The lastest poet this work discusses is Surur Alam (b. 1894).

Tulasī aur Jāyasī kī bhāṣā kā Tulanātmak Adhyayana by L. Mishra (1991) compares in detail nouns in subject, object, instrumental, and other case positions as they occur in the works of Jayasi and Tulasī. The pronouns, adjectives, and verb forms are also compared in detail.

Bhala Chandra Tiwari's *Sūfi Kāvya meṁ Nārī* (1991) focuses on the depiction of women in the poetry of Jayasi. Female characters are examined with regard to their spiritual, historical, and psychological aspects.

Scholarship Specific to the Study of Daud's Cāndāyan

Parmeshvarilal Gupta's *Cāndāyan* of 1964 was the first work to offer the text of *Cāndāyan*, a commentary, and a description of supporting research materials. The best feature of this work is the reproduction of pages from the *Cāndāyan* manuscripts from England, Bombay, Benaras, Maner, and Punjab. According to Gupta, no manuscript of *Cāndāyan* available thus far is complete. The following manuscripts form the basis of his edition:

1. The Manchester manuscript in England is in Persian script. It contains 318 folios (636 pages), some of them missing. Each page contains only one *kaḍvak*. Each page opens with a synopsis of the *kaḍvak* it contains in Persian prose. Three hundred and forty-nine pages have text and the remaining have pictures which are very significant in terms of the history of Indian painting.

2. The Bombay manuscript of the Prince of Wales Museum contains only 64 pages, which were originally brought from Bhopal. Each of these leaves have text on one side and pictures on the other. The folios have no numbers and the *kaḍvaks* written on them do not have any numeration to place them within the text as a whole. Each page contains a heading in Persian prose, providing either the gist of the following *kaḍvak* or introducing its topic. The third *yamaka* is divided into two separate lines making the *kaḍvak* a stanza of eight lines.[19] This feature of the manuscript supports the argument that the early poets of the Indo-Sufi *masnavī* were not sure about the rules of Indic prosody.
3. A manuscript belonging to Francis Hoffer, a collector in the United States, has two pages of *Cāndāyan* manuscript, resembling those of the Bombay manuscript.
4. The Maner manuscript was obtained by Hasan Askari, Professor of History at the University of Patna, from the *khanqāh* (monastery) of Maner (Bihar). It consists of 64 pages in Persian script. Basically the pages resemble those of the Bombay manuscript, but the scribes are different. The margin of each page contains a *kaḍvak* from Kutuban's *Mṛgāvatī*. The pagination, the number of the individual *kaḍvaks*, and the text of the *Cāndāyan* are not recorded in any organized fashion, creating potential confusion.
5. The Punjab manuscript from the Lahore Central Archives used to have 24 pages of *Cāndāyan* text. After Partition, India got ten pages, now in the Punjab National Archives in Patiala. P. Gupta obtained a photocopy of only ten pages out of 14 from the Lahore Archives, an indication of the deterioration of the manuscript. Each leaf contains the text of *Cāndāyan* on one side and has a picture on the other. Each page contains eight lines because the Persian prose section is written out in two lines and the third *yamaka* is divided into two lines.
6. The Kashi manuscript contains only six pages and is housed in the Bharat Kala Bhavan at Kashi University. These pages are also in Persian script and resemble the Punjab manuscript.

   None of the above-described manuscripts provide information about the dates when they were written. They are written in a style of Nastalīq calligraphy that was popular during Akbar's reign but went out of style in approximately 1550, so they have been dated between 1525 and 1570.[20]
7. The Bikaner manuscript possibly (P. Gupta is not sure because he

did not actually see this manuscript) has 438 *kaḍvaks* written in the *Kāmdarī* script of Rajasthan. The collector did not share his manuscript with Gupta and he only had access to pages that the owner had published in *Varadā*, the periodical of the Rajasthan Sahitya Samiti (2nd year, number 3, pp. 26–33).

8. In the Raza Library of Rampur, there is a manuscript of Jayasi's *Padmāvat* dated to 1674. On the cover of this manuscript under the title *Cāndāyan*, four lines of the text of *Cāndāyan* are written that are not found in any extant manuscript.

During his research P. Gupta (1964: 24–5) was given a description of several manuscripts in the possession of a number of collectors. None of these were accessible to Gupta. However, he gives a brief account of some of them in his edition of *Cāndāyan*.

Mataprasad Gupta's critical edition of *Cāndāyan* was published in 1967. It provides information about the author Daud. A detailed description of the seven manuscripts that constitute the basis for his critical edition is followed by a linguistic analysis to determine that the language of *Cāndāyan* seems to be older than that of *Padmāvat*. The information regarding the seven manuscripts, some of which had already been described in P. Gupta's 1964 edition of *Cāndāyan*, is as follows:

1. The Kashi manuscript of Bharat Kala Bhavan is #6 of P. Gupta's sources.
2. The Bikaner manuscript, dated 1673, #7 in P. Gupta's sources, formed the main source for M. Gupta's edition of *Cāndāyan*. Currently this manuscript is in Vidyapith, Agra. The significance of this manuscript can hardly be overstated because it was instrumental in establishing M. Gupta's edition as more authentic than P. Gupta's for the following reasons:
   (a) Only a few pages were available to P. Gupta, whereas M. Gupta had access to the entire manuscript.
   (b) This is the only manuscript in Devanagari script. The Devanagari script does account for all the short vowels. This is crucial for the correct reading of compositions in the Indic languages. Short vowels are not meticulously written out in the Persian Nastalīq writing system. According to Shyam Manohar Pandey, this gave the edge to the M. Gupta edition over the P. Gupta edition.[21]
   (c) Unlike the Lahore portion of the Punjab manuscript, the Bikaner manuscript is well preserved. Its legibility was of great help in

determining correct readings. The reading of many words of the text of *Cāndāyan* remained in a state of confusion due to a lack of understanding of the old style of the Nastalīq script.

(d) The Bikaner manuscript contains 439 *kaḍvaks*—in total, a very large manuscript compared to all the others.[22]

3. The Bhopal manuscript is described as the Bombay manuscript in P. Gupta's edition (#2). Currently it is in the Prince of Wales Museum in Bombay. P. Gupta had been the curator of the Museum when he began work on his edition of *Cāndāyan*.
4. The Maner manuscript, which is described as manuscript #4 in P. Gupta's edition of *Cāndāyan*.
5. The Massachusetts manuscript, which is the same as #3 in P. Gupta's edition.
6. The Manchester manuscript, which is source #1 in P. Gupta's edition.
7. and 8. The Simla manuscripts from the State Archives of Shimla are a set of ten pages from one manuscript and nine pages from another manuscript of *Cāndāyan*. The pages are not sequential. According to M. Gupta, these manuscripts are not well preserved and are somewhat illegible.
9. The Rampur manuscript. M. Gupta lists this manuscript separately from the Maner manuscript, #4 in P. Gupta's edition.

In his edition of *Cāndāyan* M. Gupta provides a somewhat more detailed description of each of the manuscripts that had already been described by P. Gupta.

Gyan Chandra Sharma's *Cāndāyan kā Sāṁskṛtik Pariveś* was published in 1973. To my knowledge, this is one of the earliest of the secondary sources exclusively dedicated to the study of *Cāndāyan*. Its focus is the religious, spiritual, and cultural aspects of life as depicted in the text. It traces the Hindu beliefs and practices described that figure therein. The detailed explanations of the social customs, layouts of the cities, foods, apparel, cosmetics, ornaments, musical instruments, coins, and units of measurement make this an interesting study.

Shyam Manohar Pandey published his *The Hindi Oral Epic Loriki* in 1979. It contains the various regional oral versions of the folktale *Lorikī*, the inspiration for *Cāndāyan*.

Shahnaz Parveen's *Cāndāyan kā Sānskṛtik Adhyayana* (1985) traces Indian and Western Asiatic customs found in *Cāndayan*. *The Siddhu* and *Nātha* cult and Islamic practices are also discussed. All aspects of the social and cultural life referred to in *Cāndāyan* are illustrated.

Shyam Manohar Pandey's *Hindī aur Fārsi Sūfi Kāvya* (1989) contains eight articles on the subject of the *masnavī* genre. However, the first 57 pages provide information that is crucial for the study of *Cāndāyan*.

To my knowledge, thus far, but a few of the Indo-Sufi *masnavīs* have been translated into any European language in their entirety. Why is it that the Indo-Sufi *masnavī* literature has largely been studied and discussed in a serious way during only the last fifty years? Secondly, given the extraordinary volume of the Indo-Sufi *masnavī* literature, why has it been, with some exceptions, virtually unknown to scholars in the West? The answer lies in the socio-political climate of twentieth-century India, in particular, the decades just before and after Partition.

At this point, a look at the socio-political background against which the classification and periodization of Hindi literature took place is of crucial importance. Persian was the court language during the centuries of Muslim rule. During the British Raj, Urdu gradually gained supremacy and Persian faded away. When Hindi gained importance towards the second quarter of the twentieth century and was later declared the national language, scholars of Hindi literature organized the available material according to chronological order and subject.

Moreover, Indo-Sufi *masnavī* literature did not fit neatly into a set chronological time-frame. The great volume of Indo-Sufi *masnavī* literature, much of which was still being discovered, was somewhat problematic in terms of its place in the history of Hindi literature *vis-à-vis* the content of the genre, as well as the fact that most authors who had composed *masnavīs* in Hindi were Muslim. The fact that Indo-Sufi literature was written mainly in Perso-Arabic script meant that *masnavīs* were largely out of reach of those who were not familiar with the writing system. This was especially true if the reader could not read handwriting that was in the style of several hundred years ago. This made Indo-Sufi literature different by comparison with all the other Hindi literature.

The result of not being able to read Persian script and of not being able to understand the meaning of the *surkhiyān* (literally the rubrics, which were in Persian prose, at least in the case of *Cāndāyan*) was not surprising. Without really having read *masnavī* literature in any detail, Hindi scholars of the old school viewed it as a kind of literature that was not quite Indian because they thought that it clearly followed in the footsteps of the Persian *masnavī*. Perhaps the inaccessibility of the material kept many historians of Hindi literature unsure about what to make of it.

The allegation that our understanding of Indo-Sufi *masnavīs* has been hampered by a lack of consideration of the specifically Sufi context for these works is supported by the comments of earlier scholars. Pathak's statement in support of Chaturvedi is illustrative:

> Parashuram Chaturvedi is right in saying that, in the context of Hindi literature, we cannot give much importance to the Sufi love narratives. These narratives were initiated as an introduction to a certain kind of literature with peculiar tendencies. And even later, parallel to other compositions, these compositions continued to be written in approximately the same style. The subject of this literature was selected according to the mandates dictated for the Persian *masnavīs* and their aim remained consistent with the goals of the Persian *masnavī* literature. (Pathak 1978: 72)

It is irrelevant at this point whether early scholars writing on the history of Hindi literature decided to deliberately or inadvertantly suppress or ignore the study of Indo-Sufi *masnavī* literature (because it had 'peculiar tendencies' not worthy of attention). The same body of scholars that made this decision trained, in turn, the scholars of the next generation. For example, Shukla, appointed head of the Hindi Department at the Kashi Hindu Vishvavidhyalaya in 1919, continued to organize materials and write his version of the history of Hindi literature for the next twenty years. Here is what Bachchan Singh writes in this regard:

> I never would have mustered the courage to comment (adversely) on Shukla's 'History' but for the encouragement of such a respected author as Namwar Singh. The foundation of Shukla's brand of 'History' has penetrated so deeply. What he has written, over the years, has become so unanimously and unquestionably accepted as being the absolute truth that it is an enormous challenge for the critical reader to sift through the material layer by layer to find the facts. (Singh 1989: 1–13)

The rise of literacy in the Devanagari script can be said to have coincided with the gathering momentum of the freedom struggle. After Independence and Partition, Hindi became the official language of India, and Urdu lost favour. As a result, in the past few decades, a generation of scholars has emerged who have access only to Hindi literature written in Devanagari. There are very few scholars who have complete mastery over both the Persian and the Devanagari scripts. In his *History of Hindi Literature*, Jindal writes:

It is surprising that 'scarcely a line' of *Padmavat* 'is intelligible' to Grierson (Grierson, *The Modern Vernacular Literature of Hindustan*, p. 15). Grierson's difficulty must have been not one of the language but of the script. There is no provision in the Persian alphabet to faithfully produce the diphthong sounds of Hindi nor are there so many intonations of vowel sounds. Hindi words cannot properly be written into Persian script, and an 'ordinary scholar' must surely find some difficulty in getting the hang of the matter. In 1911, G.A. Grierson in collaboration with Pandit Sudhakar Dwivedi, brought forth an authorized edition of the *Padmavat* in the Devanagari script. It is well that the Sufis wrote in the Persian script; thereby their works have been preserved to our day in their original form and are useful sources of information about the language and thought of the people of those times; *Pṛthvīrāj Rāso*, the *Śabads* and *Sākhis* of Kabir, or the lyrics of Vidyāpati and Mīrā cannot claim that authenticity due to constant changes introduced in the text by later day redactors. (Jindal: 1993: 42)

Referring to Indo-Sufi *masnavī* literature, Raṁchandra Shukla complained that the stories did not conform to Indian standards of morality. According to him, the plot was often substandard—a married prince falls in love with another women, leaves his first wife and responsibilities, and takes off in search of his love. Shukla states that the Indo-Sufi *masnavī* literature is not a literature that calls for attention. Moreover, even the prosody was considered to be Persian. The theory that the Indo-Sufi *masnavīs* were composed in the same set of meters as the Persian *masnavīs* was generally accepted by scholars until the research of Dwivedi was published (Pandey 1982: 7). The issue of prosody is important and it will be discussed in detail in a separate chapter.

As a result of all the factors mentioned above, the promotion and study of Indo-Sufi *masnavī* literature in India remained in a general state of neglect for a considerable period of time. This accounts for the long time it has taken scholars to rediscover the Indo-Sufi *masnavī*.

Modern scholars of Hindi literature, such as Mataprasad Gupta, Parmeshvarilal Gupta, Shiva Kumar Shandilya, Shyam Manohar Pandey, Shiva Sahay Pathak, and Shrinivas Batra, among others, have worked hard to counter the earlier trend. They find the *masnavī* an intriguing genre because of its scope and complexity and the diversity of its components and characteristics. A vast geographical region is involved in its birth and growth. This is reflected in the richness of its linguistic features. A study of the early compositions allows scholars a glimpse of that time when the rise of the Indo-Sufi *masnavī* can be observed.

NOTES

1. I discuss the topic of the *masnavī* in the Persian tradition later in this study. For a more detailed study, see E.G. Browne 1902 and 1928.
2. For more information on the subject of the *masnavī* genre in Turkic literature, see Vakfi 1922.
3. See Schomer and McLeod 1987.
4. In *An Outline of the History of Hindi Literature* (1982) Ram Prasad Mishra lumps together all the poetic literature composed in the fourteenth to sixteenth centuries under the rubric, 'The Period of Renaissance' (Mishra 1982).
5. The discussion at the end of this chapter includes the dates of the Indo-Sufi *masnavī* compositions of the northern recension. Table 1.1 provides the names of the writers, their works, and the approximate dates of the *masnavīs* they composed.
6. Within the limited scope of this work it is impossible to do justice to the discussion of the southern recension of Indo-Sufi *masnavī* literature. I touch upon the southern branch briefly. For additional information, see Jindal 1993: 43 and H.F. Eaton's *Sufis of Bijapur*, 1978. Peter Gaeffke's research on this topic is also noteworthy (1989).
7. In Chapter 2 I present the different views that prominent scholars of *Cāndāyan* have about the use of the term 'Awadhi'. This controversy arises in part, in my opinion, from professional rivalry. Most scholars agree that the northern recension of Indo-Sufi *masnavī* literature is composed in Awadhi, the easternmost dialect of Hindi. See Gaeffke 1994: 255.
8. Sometimes a *soraṭhā* makes up the last two lines of the *kaḍvak* unit instead of a *dohā*. Similar to the *dohā, soraṭhā* is a kind of couplet in which the first half lines contain 11 morae, or metrical units, and rhyme, and the second halflines 13 morae.
9. In his *Ācārya Śukla kā Itihās paṛhte hue* (1989: 1–14), Bachchan Singh discusses in detail the giant literary figure that Ram Chandra Shukla was, even during his lifetime, his background, the significant posts he held, his work for the Nagari Pracharini Sabha at Varanasi, the complexity of his writings, and his cultivation of a group of scholars who followed and imitated him blindly without ever having questioned his opinions. If it were not for the encouragement of scholars such as Namwar Singh, he says, he would not have dared to write his book, which expresses opinions not in agreement with Shukla's.
10. *History of Classical Urdu Literature*, M. Sadiq 1964: 39. For additional details on the subject of Persian prosody, see *Tarh-i-urūz-i-Fārasī* (Sadafi 1979).
11. Kulke and Rothermund may find Nicholson's ideas and his way of expressing them dated and unacceptable. Nonetheless, his translation of Rumi's *Masnavi* is commendable. The writings of A.J. Arberry and Annemarie Schimmel on Rumi are also commendable.
12. The story of these couplets is as follows. They were composed during times that were difficult for those who had just come to India from Iran and Central

Asia. Immigrants faced great language problems and, in order to familiarize themselves with Hindi synonyms, Amir Khusrau selected the most frequent vocabulary items from the Perso-Arabic register and provided Hindawi equivalents for them in verse form (Tiwari et al. 1985: 135–200).

13. In *Cāndāyan*, the title of each *kaḍvak* is in Persian prose. In subsequent Indo-Sufi *masnavīs*, this practice was dropped. This feature alone accounts for the larger number of vocabulary items in *Cāndāyan* from the Perso-Arabic register, compared with the *masnavīs* composed later.
14. For details, see *Sūfi Kāvya Vimarśa* of Shyam Manohar Pandey (S.M. Pandey 1968: 2).
15. Although many pages have been collected, *Cāndāyan* is still not available in its complete form. Therefore, it is impossible to tell if it did in fact contain a key to the symbols similar to the one provided by Jayasi for his *Padmāvat*.

    Cāndāyan, so far, is considered to be the first Indo-Islamic Sufi *masnavī*. Before the manuscripts of *Cāndāyan* came to light, it had been generally assumed that *Mṛgāvatī* was the oldest Indo-Sufi *masnavī*. In *Indian Muslims* (Mujeeb 1967), there is no mention of either Maulana Daud or *Cāndāyan*. However, the first fragments of the *Cāndāyan* manuscript had already been found in 1941. M. Gupta discusses in some detail the various manuscripts and copies now *Cāndāyan* available and their present location (1967: 42–7). Here is Shirani's description of one of the manuscripts:

    > In the Manchester manuscript, each leaf has a single stanza set in the middle of the page with decorative border-work followed by a second page of pictorial illustration. Each *kaḍvak* or stanza begins with a subtitle or rubric in Persian describing the subsequent episode. The last couplet either sums up the narrative of the entire stanza or introduces the following topic. (Shirani 1941: 74)

16. The fact that historians of Hindi literature made mistakes about the chronological placement of the Indo-Sufi *masnavī* points to the possibility that perhaps they could not read the dates provided within the respective texts. The results have been devastating in that the inaccessibility of this literature led to a false picture of the history of Hindi literature for many generations to come. This trend was checked only recently with Grierson's edition of *Cāndāyan*, published in 1896–1911 by the Asiatic Society of Bengal. In his *Hindi Sāhitya kā Itihās*, published in 1956, R.M. Shukla introduced Indo-Sufi literature, and *Padmāvat* in particular, to the general public.
17. H.P. Dviwedi in his *Hindi Sāhitya kī Bhūmikā*, published in 1975, was the first scholar to have pointed out that the prosody of the Indo-Sufi *masnavī* is based on Indic and not Persian meters, as previously believed (S.M. Pandey 1982: 7).
18. For details, see Dhar 1949: 339–40.
19. All terms relevant to the prosody of the Indo-Sufi *masnavī* genre and *Cāndāyan* in particular are discussed in detail in Chapter 3.

20. See P. Gupta's *Cāndāyan*, published in 1964, for more details on the manuscripts in question.
21. In *Sūfī Kāvya Vimarśa*, S.M. Pandey in the essay entitled *Cāndāyan ke Do Sanskaraṇ* offers a comparative study of the two editions of *Cāndāyan* in question (Pandey 1968: 27–36).
22. For a detailed description of the Bikaner manuscript, see M. Gupta's edition of *Cāndāyan* (M. Gupta 1967: 52–3).

2

Maulana Daud and His *Cāndāyan*

Textual Sources on Daud

Little reliable information has come down to us about the life of Maulana Daud. What information there is about his life is based on extremely limited sources.[1] These are the text of *Cāndāyan* itself; official documents of the Sufi orders with which Daud was associated;[2] passing references to *Cāndāyan* in Badauni's (d. 1596) *Muntakhab ut-Tawārīkh*;[3] and references in *Cāndāyan* to other contemporaneous historical personages about whom some biographical information is available.[4] Of these sources, *Cāndāyan* itself is the most important.

In the seventeenth *kaḍvak*, for instance, we learn that *Cāndāyan* was composed in Hijri 781 (AD 1379), when Firoz Shah was the Sultan of Delhi and Jauna Shah was Firoz Shah's chief minister. We find that Daud lived in a place he calls 'the nine-coloured Dalmau', located on a hill on the banks of the Ganges. Daud further indicates that Dalmau was inhabited by accomplished, sophisticated, and appreciative citizens and that Malik Mubarak, the son of the brave Malik Bayān, was the governor of the district. Here is the relevant text.

बरस सात सै होये इक्यासी
तिहि याह कबि सरसे उभासी
साहि पेरोज ढीली सुल्तानू
जौना साहि उजीरू वषानू
दलमौ नयरु बसै नवरंगा
उपरि कोट तले बहे गंगा
धरमी लोग बसहि भागवंता
गुनगाहक नागर जसवंता

मलिक बयां पुतु युध रन धीरू
मलिक ममारष तहां का मीरु
दाउद येह कबि जइ गाई मन महि लेहु बिचारि।
जुरत बोल चित राषहु टूटत लेहु संवारि।। (M. Gupta 1967: 17)

It was the year seven hundred and eighty-one
When this poet brought to light this work.
Shah Firoz was the Sultan of Delhi,
Jauna Shah, the famous minister.
The colourful city of Dalmau flourished,
With forts on hills, the Ganga flowing below.
Good, conscientious people lived there,
Sophisticated, connoisseurs of arts, well-reputed.
Malik Bayān, a scion, patient in battle.
His son, Malik Mubarak, is the local governor.
Daud recites this poem. Contemplate it in your mind.
Saving the pleasing ones, reorganize the broken locution.

P. Gupta (1964: 19) states that Dalmau is located on the banks of the Ganga, in Rai Bareilly district. The town became important in the reign of Iltutmish (1210–36).

Daud is also mentioned in passing in Shaikh Muhaddis Dehlavi's *Akhbārul Akhiyār*, written in Akbar's reign (1546–1605), which notes that Shaikh Zainuddin was the nephew, successor, and chief attendant of Nasiruddin Chiragh Dehlavi (d. 1356) and was also the teacher of Maulana Daud, the author of *Cāndāyan* (Pandey 1994: 286).

As mentioned above, another source that can be used to piece together a sketchy biography of Daud is the body of texts referred to as *malfūzāt*, which consists of records kept in the Sufi monasteries (*khānqāhs*). These records tell us nothing about Daud himself. They do, however, give information about Daud's spiritual guide, Shaikh Zainuddin, mentioned above. A lengthy tribute to Shaikh Zainuddin is found in the 9th *kaḍvak* of *Cāndāyan*. It reads:

सेष जैनदी हौं पथि लावा
धरम पंथ जिहि पापु गवावा
पाप दीन्ह है गांग बहाई
धरम नाव हौ लीन्ह चडाई
उघरे नैन हिये उजियारे
पायो लिषि नौ अक्षर कारे
पुनि मैं आखिर की सुधि पाई

तुरकी लिषि लिषि हिंदुकी गाई
जे पइये जाई सेष पसारा
पाप गए तसीकर मारा
तेहु का घरू निरमरा जिह चित रहा लुभाई।
सेष जेनदी सेवता पाप निरंतर जाई।। (M. Gupta 1967: 9)

Shaikh Jainadi has brought me to the path
Of righteousness so that my sins might be absolved;
Sins swept away in the Ganga,
I was elevated on the boat of devoutness.
Eyes opened, heart enlightened,
I managed to write the nine black letters[5]
Finally, conscious of my destiny,
In the Turkic script, I sang Hinduki.
Whosoever obtains the Shaikh's blessings
Gets his sins eliminated as criminals (are done away with).
Pristine is his abode, it engages (my) mind;
By serving Shaikh Jainadi one is cleansed of his sins continuously.

The information to be gleaned about Shaikh Zainuddin is admittedly limited. S.M. Pandey has summarized it as follows:

> The full name of Shaikh Jainadi was Zainuddin. He was the nephew and doyen of the Chishti saint Nasiruddin Charāgh Dehlavī. From the *malfūzāt*, where the Sufi saints' sermons and statements are recorded, it is evident that in addition to being the supervisor of the Delhi *Khānqah,* Shaikh Zainuddin was the personal attendant of Charāgh Dehlavī. (S.M. Pandey 1989: 11)

There are other figures mentioned in the *Cāndāyan*. These are Malik Mubarak and Malik Nathan. Mention of Malik Mubarak occurs in the 15th and the 16th *kaḍvak*, in a section in which Daud is praising his patron Jauna Shah (identifiable from the honorific title Khan-i-Jahan). The mention of Malik Nathan occurs in the 329th *kaḍvak* at the end of the second snakebite episode. Jauna Shah was himself a person about whom some information is known, since he served as (chief) minister of Firoz Shah Tughlaq (1309–88).

Inevitably, historical records provide information about Jauna Shah. So far as I know however, no additional information has been uncovered with regard to the other (see M. Gupta 1967: 3).

The above information, limited as it is, constitutes all there is as a basis for the biography of Daud. Other biographical information is much later and thus unreliable. Many authors have based their accounts on sources already mentioned by P. Gupta, M. Gupta, Pandey, and Jauhari. Al-Badayuni's chronicles are an important primary source. A contemporary of Akbar (1556–1605), Badayuni completed his *Muntakhab ut-Tawārīkh* in 1591.

> According to Al-Badayuni's *Muntakhab ut-Tawārīkh*, in 1370 Feroz Shah's prime minister Khan-i-Jahan died. His son Jauna Shah succeeded him as the prime minister. In *Cāndāyan*, the well known Hindi *masnavī*, the love of Lorik and Candā is described. This *masnavī* was composed by Maulana Daud and was dedicated to Jauna Shah. The *masnavī* was so famous throughout the region that it was deemed unnecessary to praise it. On one occasion Makhdūm Shaikh Wāiz Rabbanī read some parts of it and the listeners were immensely pleased. When some of the prominent scholars asked the Shaikh whether so much importance should be accorded to a Hindi *masnavī*, the Shaikh replied to them that the entire *masnavī* is filled with the divine truth and symbols. It is an interesting composition and in it is contained food for thought for those who love God and are spiritually inclined. It successfully explains the mystic meaning of some of the *āyāt* of the Quran and is a repository of the sweet songs of India. (M. Gupta 1967: 3)

Literary Sources and the Critical Editions of the Cāndāyan

Two prominent scholars, Parmeshvarilal Gupta and Mataprasad Gupta, have done considerable work in locating manuscripts of *Cāndāyan* and publishing detailed descriptions of these manuscripts (see Chapter 1). P. Gupta's edition of *Cāndāyan* came out in 1964; M. Gupta published his edition in 1967. These critical editions, written in Hindi, describe in detail all the known manuscripts of the work and the location, condition, and script of each. M. Gupta's study is the starting point for any scholar wishing to conduct manuscript work on the *Cāndāyan*. However, it should be pointed out that, valuable as it is, it has several weaknesses. These stem primarily from the fact that his edition is in Hindi and printed in Devanagari, which filters the text through a Hindi language perspective. The majority of early texts of *Cāndāyan* are in Perso-Arabic script. The process of transcribing manuscripts of *Cāndāyan* into a Devanagari format has introduced numerous errors and mis-interpretations.

The only way to clear up many of these misinterpretations is to go back and directly examine the original manuscripts, paying particular attention to those in the Arabic script and particularly noting cases where the original Awadhi as recorded in Perso-Arabic script is amenable to multiple interpretations.

In the edition of M. Gupta, the location, script, style of the calligraphy, the size of the pages, and the methodology applied to determine the numbers assigned to the various unnumbered pages is provided in detail. Often a picture is provided that gives the reader a chance to see what the actual manuscript looked like.

From a reading of the editions of M. Gupta and P. Gupta, is seems that the latter, was the first of the two scholars to begin work in Bombay on the *Cāndāyan*, using the manuscripts available to him at that time. Up until then, only fragments of *Cāndāyan* manuscripts had been available; however, P. Gupta found a manuscript at a museum in Manchester, England, which, though the largest, was still incomplete. This discovery gave P. Gupta more materials than had been available to other scholars. In the introductory chapter of his *Cāndāyan*, P. Gupta clearly describes his sources in detail. However, it seems that M. Gupta made efforts to get a hold of copies of the materials that were in P. Gupta's possession.[6]

It is very clear from the introductory chapter of P. Gupta's *Cāndāyan* that when he found out about these efforts, he became upset and anxious to publish his critical edition before M. Gupta's work was complete (P. Gupta 1964: 1–15). Consequently, P. Gupta's edition of *Cāndāyan* came out in 1964. However, because of problems with orthography and insufficient editing which resulted in duplication of some portions of the text (perhaps to some extent due to racing against time), this edition suffers from many incorrect readings. In the meantime, M. Gupta found a *Cāndāyan* manuscript in the Devanagari script. This discovery was of crucial importance because it overcame many of the problems which P. Gupta faced in dealing with the orthography of *Cāndāyan's* Arabic script manuscripts.

In their respective editions of *Cāndāyan*, P. Gupta and M. Gupta go into great detail about the writing style, condition, and location of the various manuscripts that they had consulted. The biggest problem both scholars faced was the orthography, which seems to stem from the fact that the manuscripts of the Indo-Sufi *masnavīs* were originally recorded in the Perso-Arabic script, which does not account for short vowels. The discovery of a manuscript in Devanagari was indeed opportune at this particular time when M. Gupta's *Cāndāyan* had not yet gone to press. Most manuscripts of Indian literature were either in private collections or in museum archives, slowly being catalogued. Knowledge of them was not public. As a result of the discovery of the above-mentioned manuscript, M. Gupta's critical edition, which came out in 1967, is more accurate than its predecessor.

In his *Sūfī Kāvya Vimarśa*, published in 1968, Shyam Manohar Pandey, a student of M. Gupta, compares and discusses the reasons for the differences between the two editions of *Cāndāyan* (S.M. Pandey 1968: 26–36). In Pandey's view, with which I agree, M. Gupta's edition is more reliable. The introductory material is very detailed and provides information on Daud's language. The extensive commentary and detailed discussion of the various readings in the different manuscripts makes this edition much richer than its predecessor. And most importantly, Pandey says (1968: 35), P. Gupta does not discuss *Cāndāyan* in the context of the Sufi literary tradition at all, treating it as if its purpose were merely to give the oral epic of *Loriki* a literary form. I agree with Pandey's analysis, and, except for the occasional reference, M. Gupta's critical edition remains my main source.

Plot

It is essential to be familiar with the story of *Cāndāyan* before a discussion on the Sufi elements in the text begins. To this end a brief outline of the plot is necessary.

The story begins in the lovely northern Indian city of Govar, boasting a royal garden, the city itself is adorned with glorious flora and fauna. Govar has palaces and forts surrounded by moats, and its markets are resplendent with all kinds of fruits, apparel, games, dances, shows, and sports. Govar is ruled over by Mahar Sahdev, who lives in a shining white palace complete with a lion-gate.[7] Living with Mahar Sahdev is his chief queen, Phūlārānī, and several other less-favoured queens.

During the rule of Mahar Sahdev, Phūlārānī gives birth to a beautiful daughter of the *Padminī* category.[8] This girl is actually an *avatāra* of the moon (Cānd). When she is but a year old, the tales of her beauty spread throughout the coastal regions of India, as well as in Malabar, Gujarat, Tirhut, Awadh, and Badayun. Many princely families approach Mahar Sahdev for Cāndā's hand in marriage; however, when she is four years old, Jait, who belongs to the same caste as Mahar Sahdev, sends a proposal for marriage of his son Bāvan with Cāndā. Mahar Sahdev accepts this and after the wedding, which is performed with great pomp and ceremony, Cāndā is sent to live in her father-in-law's household.

Twelve years pass after Cāndā's marriage. Her husband Bāvan is very short in stature, has only one eye, lives in squalour, and is impotent. Cāndā, now sixteen, waits another year and then complains about her situation to her sister-in-law. When her mother-in-law learns of Cāndā's unhappiness, she suggests that Cāndā should send a message to her father and go back to her parents with an escort. As soon as Mahar Sahdev receives the message from Cāndā, he sends an escort to bring her home. Upon her arrival at Govar, Cāndā's friends ask her how she was being treated by her husband. Cāndā describes her trials and tribulations to her friends, giving them a hint of Bāvan's neglect. She does so in highly florid language taking the shape of a *bārahmāsā*, in which events of her life are symbolically equated with aspects of the twelve months of the year.

In the meantime, a beggar named Bajur comes to town who sings and begs for alms from door-to-door. One day when Cāndā is looking out of her window in the white palace, Bajur happens to look up. He sees her and faints. When the people of Govar who attend Bajur ask him the reason for his fainting, he answers them with a riddle and escapes from the city, fearful of retribution.

After travelling for a full month, he arrives at Jaipur, ruled by Raja Rūpcand. Pleased with Bajur's song 'Candrāvalī', Rūpcand employs Bajur to entertain him. Eventually, Bajur divulges the identity of Cāndā and describes her beauty to Rūpcand in great detail. As soon as Rūpcand hears this he orders his army to attack Govar.

Despite bad omens, Rūpcand lays siege to Govar and sends word to Mahar Sahdev that he has come to wed Cāndā. When Mahar Sahdev consults his ministers and statesmen, two great warriors, Kuṁvaru and Dhavaru, offer to lead the battle. During the battle, however, pitched against Rūpcand's brave warrior, Bānṭhā, both Kuṁvaru and Dhavaru fall. This demoralizes Mahar Sahdev's army. He sends a pleading message to Lorik for assistance. When Lorik's wife, Mainā, and mother, Kholin, learn that Lorik has agreed to help Sahdev, they are upset. Lorik cajoles them into agreeing to send him to war and proceeds to the battlefield with their consent.

Brave Lorik's presence fills Sahdev's troops with inspiration and renews their courage. A great battle ensues and Lorik cuts Bānṭhā's head off with his blade. Rūpcand flees from the battlefield, never to return. Sahdev's army puts Lorik on an elephant and parades the streets of Govar in a victory celebration. Cāndā wants to see the person who has liberated Govar. From the terrace of her palace, she sees Lorik and is overcome with emotion. It seems as if she has suffered a heatstroke.

The next day Cāndā's handmaiden, Bṛhaspati, asks her why she became emotional. Cāndā confides in her and begs her to find an occasion so that she may look upon Lorik again. With this objective in mind, Bṛhaspati suggests Cāndā ask her father, Mahar, to call for a grand victory celebration-feast to honour the great hero. A great commemoration is under way when Lorik spots Cāndā, who comes to the terrace all dressed up. As soon as he sees Cāndā, Lorik swoons.

Lorik now stays confined to his house. According to his doctors, he is lovesick, pierced by one of Kāma's arrows, which has caused him to hallucinate and mumble. By chance, Bṛhaspati happens to visit Lorik. She asks him to tell her the reason for his sickness. Lorik confides in her and implores her to arrange a meeting between Cāndā and himself. Bṛhaspati tries to explain to Lorik how jealously Cāndā is guarded and how difficult it is to meet her, but when he insists, she suggests that he visit a certain temple and live there as a renunciate. She could then try to bring Cāndā to the temple on some pretext.

For an entire year Lorik lives in a temple and eats only the roots and bulbs that grow in the wilderness. He practices austerities and continually chants Cāndā's name. Finally, on the festival of Diwali, Cāndā summons Bṛhaspati and along with sixty other friends sets out to visit the temple. By chance, her pearl necklace breaks at this time. Observing that Cāndā's friends are busy picking up the pearls and stringing them together, Bṛhaspati leads Cāndā to the shade of the temple. Meanwhile, Cāndā's friends bring her the news of the presence of a prince who has become a yogi. Cāndā goes to greet the yogi, but even as she bends her head low in greeting, the yogi faints. Cāndā returns to her palace.

By this time Lorik has stopped cohabiting with his wife, Mainā. Mainā pleads with him to resume their previous marital life, but her pleas are unheeded. To the contrary, Cāndā and Lorik pine for each other. One day, when Cāndā asks Bṛhaspati to find a way for them to meet, Bṛhaspati goes to the woods and suggests that Lorik should somehow climb up the balcony of Cāndā's living quarters. She shows Lorik the way to Cāndā's balcony. Soon after this, on a dark and rainy night, Lorik throws a scaling hook tied to a strong rope, the sound wakes up Cāndā. When she sees Lorik, she unhooks the scale. Lorik tries to throw it up many times, hoping that it will catch in the bulwark of the balcony, but each time the hook holds, Cāndā disengages it. Finally, Cāndā secures the hook to a pillar and goes to bed. Lorik climbs up the balcony and, standing in the shelter of the pillar, examines the elegance of Cāndā's bedroom. He sees that Cāndā, whose garment has slipped away, rests on a flower-bedecked bed, her breasts exposed. Lorik wishes to awaken Cāndā but he cannot find the courage to do so.

Finally, Lorik takes Cāndā's hand in his. Cāndā seizes Lorik by his hair and calls out, 'thief, thief'. No one comes to her rescue. Ostensibly

Cāndā is in distress, but secretly she is happy that nobody has responded to her calls. In the meantime, Lorik tries to convince Cāndā that he is not a thief. He tells her how much he loves her, and that he has come to see her, and to be with her, even at the risk of his own life. Cāndā then lets go of his hair and asks him to prove his identity. Lorik introduces himself as the same person who waged war against Rūpcand and liberated Govar.

Lorik tells Cāndā that from the moment he first saw her at the feast hosted by her father, Mahar Sahdev, he had been deeply in love with her. He also professes that the seed of love grew with such intensity that it appeared to reach the very heavens. Lorik explains to Cāndā that he has taken this risk because life in this world does not matter to him anymore. It seems to him as if he had already died and had come to heaven. Hearing this, Cāndā also confesses that she had fallen in love with Lorik the day she caught a glimpse of him at the victory celebration. Cāndā tells Lorik that her actions today were to test his resolve.

To Lorik, Cāndā's words seem like ambrosia. Lorik takes hold of Cāndā's hem, but, right then, her pearl necklace breaks. She asks Lorik to pick up the pearls. By then it is dawn. Cāndā hides Lorik under her bed for the day. The next night, when Cāndā and Lorik are together again, Lorik describes to her all the trials and sacrifices he has undergone to find her. This night their love finds fulfilment.

Next morning, when Cāndā's maids come to help her dress, they see her broken bodice and notice the marks of lovemaking on her body. They tell Cāndā that it appears that she has experienced the joys of physical love, that 'the honey bee has entered the bud' [भंवर फूल पर बइठेउ लाग दीख तेहि अंग]. However, Cāndā makes some excuses about not having been able to sleep all night. When Cāndā's family comes to see her that day, out of embarrassment and from fear of being detected, bashful Cāndā refuses to see them. Cāndā's parents are upset and afraid for their honour. To Lorik, who is hiding right there, a dishonourable death seems inevitable. Upon nightfall, both Cāndā and Lorik renew their pledges to remain faithful to each other, and Cāndā creates a diversion to enable Lorik to escape.

When Mainā, Lorik's wife, asks him where he had spent the previous night, Lorik makes excuses. Rumours linking Lorik and Cāndā have by this time spread, causing Mainā to suspect infidelity. Nonetheless, Lorik successfully convinces Mainā of his loyalty to her.

In the meantime, all of Govar prepares to celebrate the upcoming festival of Somnāth. Women, dressed in their best, set out to the temple to worship. Cāndā also goes there with her sixty handmaidens. As she prays for a reunion with Lorik, Mainā arrives at the temple with her sixty attendants to pray for the total destruction of the woman who had snatched her husband from her. Triggered, initially, by an exchange of taunting and acerbic remarks, a physical fight erupts between the two women, which in its bloody ferocity threatens to destroy the serenity of the very gods who witness it.

At last, Lorik arrives and brings the two women to their senses. When Cāndā returns home in disgrace, she moans that she has been insulted. Mainā, on the other hand, complains to her mother-in-law, Kholin, that because of Lorik's intervention, Cāndā managed to escape. Mainā, otherwise, had been determined to tear Cāndā clothes off. In anger, Kholin sends a sarcastic message to Cāndā's mother, who, in turn, reprimands Cāndā.

Unable to bear the censure of the townspeople, Cāndā sends Bṛhaspati with a message to Lorik to the effect that if he does not come to elope with her that night, she will take poison the next morning. Lorik has an astrologer calculate the most auspicious moment to travel and, accordingly, the next day at midnight, he helps Cāndā out of her palace. On the way, Lorik stops to say farewell to his brother, Kuṁvaru. When Kuṁvaru learns of his decision, he is greatly distressed and tries to dissuade Lorik. Nevertheless, Lorik and Cāndā, dressed in disguise, proceed on their way to cross the Ganga.

The news of the elopement spreads like wildfire throughout the region. Lorik and Cāndā are about to cross the Ganga when Bāvan, Cāndā's lawfully wedded husband, comes in hot pursuit. In the course of the inevitable struggle which follows, Bāvan shoots three arrows at Lorik, but Lorik successfully fends off all three. Frustrated and mortified, Bāvan curses that a snake should bite Cāndā as a just reward for her conduct.

Bāvan returns to Govar, while Lorik and Cāndā continue on their journey past Kalinga (part of modern Orissa) to the town of Hardi Patan, where Lorik intends to visit some kinsmen. On the way, they have several experiences, some dangerous and some pleasant. It is a full-moon night when they arrive at a Brahmin's home and settle down for the night. They make themselves a flower bed to rest upon. In the night, attracted by the fragrance of the flowers, a snake comes and bites Cāndā. Lorik is tormented with anguish. However, a *gāruḍī* (a person who administers mantras against snakebites) happens to be passing. He revives Cāndā with his mantras. Lorik offers his jewellery to the *gāruḍī*, but the *gāruḍī* asks for additional valuables and gets them. Lorik and Cāndā are thankful for their stroke of good fortune.

The next evening, they take shelter under a large leafy tree to rest for the night. Near the early hours of dawn, Cāndā succumbs to a second snakebite. Lorik laments for Cāndā for two days and nights. At last, he prepares a funeral pyre of sandalwood and, holding her to his shoulder, he wishes to ignite the fire when another *gāruḍī* comes by. Lorik implores him to revive Cāndā. This time, he compensates the *gāruḍī* with his own weapons and all the valuables that Cāndā was wearing.

When finally Lorik and Cāndā arrive at Hardi Patan, Lorik is dismayed to discover that he does not know anyone there. He is a total stranger to the inhabitants of the region; however, the local king offers Lorik and Cāndā hospitality and they happily live there.

Back in Govar, Mainā and Kholin are inconsolable in Lorik's absence and continue to ask travellers all kinds of questions. After some time, Mainā sends a message to Lorik, begging him to return to Govar. When Lorik receives Mainā's message and hears from the messenger how his family has suffered after his departure from Govar, he weeps. To Cāndā's bitter regret, Lorik prepares to return with her to Govar.

As Lorik nears Govar, he stops a short distance from the city. The inhabitants of Govar suspect that they might be attacked by the newcomer. They begin to strengthen their fortifications and moats in anticipation of a battle. However, for no obvious reason, Mainā starts to feel a sense of relief in her heart which was always burning. Lorik entices Mainā to visit his tent, where, still in disguise, he begins a conversation with her to test her chastity. He is satisfied.

In the course of the conversation, Mainā recognizes Cāndā and once again a physical fight between the two occurs. Lorik, however, cajoles both of them to make peace. He begs Mainā's forgiveness for the pain he has caused her. All of them arrive in Govar where Lorik's mother, Kholin, welcomes both Mainā and Cāndā.

Lorik is shocked to see the deplorable condition to which Mainā and Kholin had been reduced in his absence. He asks his mother where his brother Kuṁvaru is. Kholin tells him that when the news of Lorik's elopement with Cāndā spread throughout the region, Cāndā's father, Sahdev, sent men to take over Lorik's livestock. Kuṁvaru was treacherously killed by Sahdev's men. Sahdev had rejoiced when he heard of Kuṁvaru's assassination. Kholin tells Lorik of the unbearable sorrow she had been forced to endure, which deprived her of sleep in the night and did not let her live during the day.

At this point the *Cāndāyan* narrative stops. On the basis of the oral *Loriki* material, one may guess that, following the tradition of brave warriors, Lorik would not have rested until he had avenged the death of his brother and restored his property to its former glory. According to one recension of *Loriki*, when Lorik challenged his brother's killer to a fight, he came out the victor. According to another recension, Lorik was killed in the struggle and Cāndā and Mainā commit *satī* on his funeral pyre. In the absence of further text, however, we can only conjecture, but never be certain, how Daud's *masnavī* actually came to conclude.

The plot of *Cāndāyan*, described above, has been divided by M. Gupta into 27 parts, as follows:

1.	स्तुति खन्ड	Devotional portion
2.	गोवर वर्णन खन्ड	Description of Govar
3.	चान्दा जन्म एवं विवाह	Birth and marriage of Cāndā
4.	चान्दा पितृगृह आगमन	Cāndā's return to her father's house
5.	बाजुर-मूर्छा खन्ड	Fainting of Bajur
6.	चान्दा श्रृंगार खन्ड	Description of Cāndā's adornment
7.	गोवर अभियान खन्ड	Attack on Govar
8.	गोवर युद्ध खन्ड	War at Govar
9.	प्रथम दर्शन खन्ड	Lorik and Cāndā: The first sight
10.	पुनर्दर्शन खन्ड	Lorik and Cāndā see each other again
11.	धवलगृह आरोहण	Lorik climbs up the terrace
12.	चांदा लोर संवाद खन्ड	Dialogue between Lorik and Cāndā
13.	चांदा लोर मिलन खन्ड	Union of Lorik and Cāndā
14.	मैना समाधान खन्ड	Pacifying Mainā
15.	चांदा मैना विवाद	Argument between Cāndā and Mainā
16.	परदेश प्रस्थान खन्ड	Lorik and Cāndā leave the country
17.	कुंवरु भेंट खन्ड	Lorik meets his brother Kuṁvaru
18.	बावन युद्ध खन्ड	Struggle with Bāvan
19.	कलिंग युद्ध खन्ड	War at the Kalinga region
20.	प्रथम सर्पदंश खन्ड	First snakebite episode
21.	द्वितीय सर्पदंश खन्ड	Second snakebite episode
22.	हरदी-पाटन निवास	Living at the Hardi Patan region
23.	मैना-संदेश-निवेदन	Mainā's message of entreaty
24.	संदेश-प्राप्ति स्वदेशागमन	Receiving message, returning home
25.	मैना सतीत्व परीक्षा	The testing of Mainā's chastity
26.	गृह आगमन खन्ड	Homecoming episode
27.	अन्त खन्ड	The concluding portion

Language

Scholars differ in their opinions regarding the name and linguistic character of the dialect of Hindi in which *Cāndāyan* is composed. There are two main schools of thought, two views as to the term that is to be applied in referring to the language of *Cāndāyan*. One of these has been advocated by Ramchandra Shukla (1965: 75–6), Dwivedi (1975: 58–9), M. Gupta (1967: 72), and S.M. Pandey (1982: 290), who identify the language of the text as Awadhī. The other view, espoused primarily by P. Gupta (P. Gupta 1964: 34), refers to the language as Hindawi.

In his *Evolution of Awadhi*, Baburam Saksena defines Awadhī as follows:

> Awadhī is the main dialect of the Eastern Hindi branch of the Indo-Aryan group of languages spoken in Northern India. The term Awadhī appears to denote the language of Awadh, but, as a matter of fact, the language is not confined to the province of Oudh. In the districts of Lakhimpur, Sitapur, Lucknow, Unao, Fatehpur, Bahraich, Barabanki, Rae Bareli, Gonda, Fyzabad, Sultanpur, Partabgarh, Allahabad, Jaunpur and Mirzapur, Awadhī is spoken in its Western, Central, and Eastern varieties. Other forms of Awadhī such as Bagheli, Tiharī, Gahora and Mandalāhi or Chattisgaṛhi, in the south, are mutually intelligible. (Saksena 1937: 3)

Regarding the origin of the Awadhī language, Saksena differs from Grierson, who connects Eastern Hindi with Ardhamāgadhī. According to Saksena, 'Awadhī has more affinity with Pālī than with Ardhamāgadhī. *Mṛgāvatī*, a romantic poem written in 1512 AD by Qutḅan in the reign of Sher Shah's father Husein Shah, is possibly the earliest extant work in Awadhī' (Saksena 1937: 1–10).[9]

Saksena also discusses the question of the antiquity of Awadhī. He equates the language of *Mṛgāvatī*, a *masnavī* written in 1512 by Kutuban in the reign of Sher Shah's father Hussain Shah, with Awadhī (Saksena 1937: 15).

M. Gupta, for his part, writes the following: 'In order to get a clearer picture of the linguistic peculiarities of the language of *Cāndāyan*, I compare it with the language of the *Ukti-vyakti-prakaraṇa*, a composition by Damodar which happens to be two hundred years older than *Cāndāyan*' (M. Gupta 1967: 61).

Suniti Kumar Chatterji, who introduces the standard text of the *Ukti-vyakti-prakaraṇa*, refers to the language of that text as Old Kosalī, which he clearly prefers to Old Awadhī. Gupta appropriates Chatterji's characterization of the language of the *Ukti-vyakti-prakaraṇa* in describing the language of *Cāndāyan*. Gupta writes, 'According to Suniti Kumar

Chatterji, the language of *Ukti* is derived from Sanskrit, and is a forerunner of Kosalī, otherwise known as Awadhī. Simultaneously, I compare the language of *Cāndāyan* with that of Jayasi's *Padmāvat*, a composition approximately two hundred years older than *Cāndāyan* (M. Gupta 1967: 61).

After providing an analysis of noun, pronoun, and adjective forms in *Cāndāyan*, M. Gupta concludes,

> Out of the hundred forms that have been compared, it seems that in only four to six cases the linguistic forms of *Cāndāyan* are different from the forms of the *Ukti vyakti prakaraṇa*. Clearly Daud's language seems to be similar to or, in some cases, a more developed form of the language of the *Ukti*. Although it is similar to the language used by Jayasi, it seems to be somewhat more archaic in form. (M. Gupta 1967: 72)[10]

A complicating factor in the argument concerning the identity of the language of *Cāndāyan* has been a dispute between scholars as to the accuracy of the language appearing in various published editions. In particular, S.M. Pandey (1968: 32) has criticised the reliability of discussions based on P. Gupta's reconstruction of the text. He alleges that P. Gupta has made countless errors in the process of reconstructing grammatical forms. Pandey greatly prefers that linguistic discussion of *Cāndāyan* be based on M. Gupta's edition of the text and accepts M. Gupta's identification of the language of *Cāndāyan* as a type of fourteenth-century Awadhī. Continuing his argument, Pandey speculates as to why Daud and other Sufi poets of northern India used the Awadhī dialect for their *masnavī* compositions.

> Mulla Daud, who is considered a pioneer poet of the Sufi Romance tradition, was a resident of Dalmau, which is in the Rae Bareli district. Awadhi is the language spoken in this region. Perhaps in order to cultivate a wider range of audiences for their (Sufi) message, the Sufi saints decided to compose their *masnavīs* in the lingua franca. It is a well-recorded fact that, during their discourses, Nizamuddin Aulia and his spiritual masters before him spoke in Hindawi language (later named Awadhi). Many of Amir Khusrau's (d. 1325) compositions are in the Awadhi language. After making India their home, it is hardly surprising that the Sufi poets adopted the regional dialect to compose their *masnavīs*. Awadhi was the most suitable choice because the subject matter of their compositions was often inspired by the local folklore. (S.M. Pandey 1961: 290)

However, P. Gupta argues that R. Shukla's identification of the language of the Sufi romances with Awadhi has been uncritically accepted. He also criticises the view of Pandey, that equates the language of *Cāndāyan* with that of an eleventh-century Apabhraṁśa text, *Rāula Vela*, ascribed to Roṛā. Pandey based his view on the published edition of *Rāula Vela* prepared by his teacher, M. Gupta. There, M. Gupta designates the language of *Rāula Vela* as a southern dialect of Kosalī, which he in turn considers to be a subtype of Awadhi (M. Gupta 1963(a): 23). P. Gupta finds Pandey's argument unconvincing and says the language is a form of Hindawi. A major portion of his reasoning is as follows:

> Regarding the language of *Cāndāyan*, Shyam Manohar Pandey mentions another poetic composition of the eleventh century, namely *Rāula Vela*, written by Roṛā. Part of the collection of the Prince of Wales Museum of Bombay, it is an incomplete composition, etched on the flat surface of a stone. Mataprasad Gupta has published a reading of *Rāula Vela* in *Hindi Anuśīlan* in which he has declared the language of *Rāula Vela* to be the Kosali of a southern branch. S.M. Pandey declares that the discovery of *Rāula Vela* and its linguistic analysis makes our task of gaining insight into the language of *Cāndāyan* easier. Now we can easily deduce that in the early centuries of the present millennium, poetic compositions were being written in a southern branch of Kosali, which is a form of Awadhi. (P. Gupta 1964: 34)

P. Gupta continues,

> Pandey writes with complete conviction that Awadhi was the language of the Dalmau region. Daud must have chosen Awadhi in order to cultivate a wider audience. Traditionally, the Sufi poets had been partial to the language of their region. Consequently, the Sufi poets living in the Punjab region composed *Sassi-Punno* and *Hīr-Rānjhā* in the Punjabi language. Similarly Daulat Qazi and other poets who resided in Bengal composed their works in Bangla. I am surprised that the fact that *Cāndāyan* was neither composed in an Awadhi environment nor was it initially recited for the benefit of the Awadhi speaking public, was completely ignored. . . .
>
> *Cāndāyan*, as is clearly stated by Abdul Qadir Badayuni, was composed in honor of Jauna Shah, the prime minister of Delhi. Shaikh Rabbani used to recite parts of it for the general public from the pulpit. Obviously, *Cāndāyan* was composed in a language which could be understood by the prime minister as well as by the local population. Badayuni clearly states that the language of *Cāndāyan* is Hindawi. He must have used the term 'Hindawi' to define that language which was contemporarily used by the Sufi saints during their discourses and was easily understood by nobility and public alike. Therefore, Awadhi is not an appropriate name for this language because it is confining in its geographical scope. (P. Gupta 1964: 32)

P. Gupta then presents his own comparative analysis of the linguistic forms of *Ukti* and *Cāndāyan* and concludes:

If Awadhī be the language of *Ukti*, then the linguistic features of *Cāndāyan* do not bear any resemblance with the former. On the basis of the present analysis I declare that M. Gupta as well as S.M. Pandey both are wrong in their thesis. Only after a more detailed and scientific study of the linguistic features of *Cāndāyan* could we arrive at the right conclusion. (P. Gupta 1964: 31–5)

Given the seeming discrepancies in the characterizations of the language of *Cāndāyan* that refer to it variously as Awadhī, Old Kosalī, Hindawi, etc., one might conclude that there is substantive disagreement as to the empirical characteristics of the text under discussion. This is not the case, however. In fact, this seeming disagreement is about terminology only and has little to do with matters of phonology, morphology, and syntax.

It is well known that the phonological and morphological inventories of early NIA texts vary greatly, and even closely related manuscripts of the same text often show points of linguistic difference.

What, then, is the most appropriate way of placing the language of *Cāndāyan* on a linguistic map of early NIA literary languages? It is clear that the speech form in question, in both the published editions of P. Gupta and of M. Gupta, is an early form of an eastern Hindi dialect variously referred to as Awadhī, Kosalī, etc. Although there are some general similarities to the language of both *Ukti-vyakti-prakaraṇa* and *Rāula Vela*, these similarities are mostly superficial. A more substantial equation is with the language of later *masnavī* texts, most particularly that of *Padmāvat*. We are fortunate in that Lakshmi Dhar, in his excellent 1949 edition and study of the work, has provided us with the tools for describing the language of the text. His work, which is based upon six manuscripts dated as early as 1969, contains a grammatical sketch and a complete index verborum. By comparing grammatical forms and vocabulary in published editions of *Cāndāyan* with the grammatical and other linguistic information given by Lakshmi Dhar, one can be confident in stating that if the language of *Cāndāyan* and *Padmāvat* are not identical, they at least occupy the same linguistic universe.

A detailed grammatical analysis of *Cāndāyan* language is beyond the scope of this dissertation, and it would not be productive to give a full morphological inventory of forms occurring in *Cāndāyan*. Rather, I shall confine myself to a summary (see tables 2.1, 2.2 and 2.3) of some of the more noticeable morphological features evident in *Cāndāyan*. For this summary, I rely heavily on materials described by M. Gupta (1967: 60–72).[11]

The verbal system of *Cāndāyan* differs in few significant respects

Table 2.1. Morphological Features of Nouns

Case	Singular[1/]	Plural[1/]	Singular[1/]	Plural[1/]	Post-Position
Nominative (kartā)	-a (-u)	-a (-u)	-a (-u)	-a (-u)	–
Objective (karma)	-a (-u)	-a (-u)	-a (-u)	-a (-u)	–
Instrumental (karaṇa)	(-aiṁ)	–	-nha[2/]	-nha[2/]	seuṁ, setiṁ, saiṁ
Dative (saṁpradāna)	-hi	-hi	–	–	kahaṁ, lāgi
Adlative (apādāna)	–	–	–	–	huta
Genitive (saṁbandha)	-kar	-ke	-ka (-kai)	-ke	–
Locative (adhikaraṇa)	-a(-i)	-aiṁ	-a (i)	-aiṁ	manjh
Vocative (saṁbodhana)	-a or -e[3/]	-a or -e[3/]	-a or -e[3/]	-a or -e[3/]	–

[1/] Parentheses indicate inflectional suffixes

[2/] Variations of -nha may also occur.

[3/] *Re* occurs before or after nouns in the vocative case.

Table 2.2. Morphological Features of Pronouns

	Singular			Plural			
Pronoun	1st	2nd	3rd	1st	2nd	3rd	Post-Position
Nominative	maiṁ	taiṁ, tū, tuma	so	hauṁ			
Objective	mohi		tehiṁ			setem, setim	tehi
Dative	mohi		tehiṁ			setem, setim	tehi
Genitive	mora (m), tor mori (f)			hamār			

from that of *Padmāvat,* as studied by Dhar (1949). *Cāndāyan's* verb system has been studied by both P. Gupta and M. Gupta, although the P. Gupta's analysis has been criticised by S.M. Pandey (1982) on methodological grounds. The particular configuration of competing suffixes for any particular verbal category does not dovetail exactly with that of *Padmāvat*, but the sets of variants in the two works

Table 2.3. Morphological Features of Demonstratives, Reflexives, Interrogatives, and Adjectives

	Singular		Plural	
	Masculine	Feminine	Masculine	Feminine
Proximate Demonstratives[1/]	eha	ehi, ehiṁ	eha	ehi, ehiṁ
Remote Demonstratives[1/]	so, teiṁ, tehiṁ	so, teiṁ, tehiṁ	so, teiṁ, tehiṁ	so, teiṁ, tehiṁ
Reflexive	–	apanī[2/]	–	apanī[2/]
Interrogatives	kavana	kavani	kavane	keiṁ
Adjectives[3/]	-a	-i	-a	-i

[1/] Indicative form.
[2/] Occurs in feminine form only.
[3/] Exceptions to these suffixes occurs when changes are dictated by the metrics.

nevertheless, are sufficiently close to all the verbal systems of the two works to be considered as essentially the same.

A detailed examination of the linguistic features of *Cāndāyan* is needed. In its vast scope, such a project would itself constitute a great and interesting undertaking. However, it should necessarily be a separate and independent work. Lakshmi Dhar's *Padumavati* (1949) is a model for such a study. Saksena's *Evolution of Awadhi* (1971) and S.K. Chatterji's work on Damodar's *Ukti-vyakti-prakaraṇa* would certainly be of great help in such a proposed project. It will be impossible to justify extensive discussion of the linguistic features of *Cāndāyan* within the compass of the project at hand.

Thus, as was the case for *Padmāvat* (Dhar 1949: 18), the verbal system in *Cāndāyan* can be seen to comprise the present, the future, and the past in the indicative mood and the present and the future in the imperative mood. In addition, the text displays the use of periphrastic tenses formed with combinations of participial forms of main verbs with inflected forms of auxiliary verbs.

In conclusion, what makes the study of the language of *Cāndāyan* interesting is that it represents a transitional phase. This is a very significant feature from the standpoint of linguistics. The postpositional system, a distinguishing feature of modern Hindi, is not yet consistently in place. However, the inflectional system is also observed in the language of *Cāndāyan*.

NOTES

1. What little information is available has been reported in publications by P. Gupta (1964), M. Gupta (1967), S.M. Pandey (1968, 1979, 1989), and Jauhari (1990).
2. It has been a traditional practice of Sufi monasteries (*khānqāhs*) to maintain extensive administrative records, collectively referred to as *malfūzāt* (literally, records). Within the *malfūzāt* of a particular *khānqāh*, the sermons of the presiding shaikh are recorded. A discussion of the use of *malfūzāt* as sources of historical, social, and political information is given in Rizvi (1975: 1–17).
3. The standard edition of Badauni is Ranking (1976). Biographical information on Badauni is contained in Beale (1971: 4).
4. Biographical information on Sufi saints, some of whom were contemporaries of Daud, and one of whom, Shaikh Zainuddin, was Daud's spiritual preceptor (pīr), is contained in Mohaddis Dehlavi's (d. 1692) *Akhbārul Akhiyār*. Dehlavi was a contemporary of Akbar. Pandey discusses the aforementioned text in which information regarding Daud is contained (1968: 2). Other discussions of Daud's contemporaries can be found in S.M. Pandey (i978 and 1982), Jauhari (1990: 159), G. Sharma (1973: 1–10), P. Gupta (1964: 19–20) and M. Gupta (1967: 1–3).
5. The meaning of the phrase 'nine black letters' (नौ अक्षर कारे) is not clear. The phrase undoubtedly stems from the practice of attributing esoteric meaning to individual letters of the Arabic alphabet. For a discussion of the Islamic practices of interpreting letters (*ilm-i-abjad*), see Bakhtiar (1976: 114) and Schimmel (1994: 113–76).
6. P. Gupta's *Cāndāyan* (1964: 6–15).
7. *Siṁha-dvār*, literally lion-gate, is a common architectural feature of many regal buildings in Asia and elsewhere symbolizing royal splendour. Either the gate to the garden which surrounds the palace or the actual palace building has two huge statues of lions on either side of its doors, as if guarding them.
8. A woman of beauty and accomplishment, hence belonging in the first of four traditional classes of women.
9. This observation is understandable because the existence of *Cāndāyan* was not known until the early 1940s.
10. M. Gupta's edition of *Cāndāyan* (1967) offers a detailed comparative study of the language of *Ukti*, *Cāndāyan*, and *Padmāvat*. The information provided here is only a summary.
11. At the very beginning of his discussion of the language of the composition, Mata Prasad Gupta states, 'Like many issues concerning Daud, his language also is a controversial issue.' To see an analysis of the adjectival forms from the 'Second Snakebite Episode' of the composition, M.P. Gupta refers us to the Newsletter of the Agra Vidyapith 'Bharatiya Sahita' (no issue number or details are provided in the footnote 86). The article 'Dauda kı Bhasha', according to M.P. Gupta is 'prakashaniya', worthy of publication (Gupta 1967: 60).

3

Structure of the Indo-Sufi *Masnavī*

General Structure

Subsequent to the *masnavī* compositions of Amir Khusrau (d. 1325), Indo-Sufi *masnavī* literature gradually evolved to establish a separate identity away from its Persian roots. These changes were evident not merely in the change of language, but also in the selection of subject matter; in the description of scenes, rituals, and festivals; and, above all, in the incorporation of features typical of the indigenous literary traditions.

Discussing the process of indigenization in literature, Ali Asani (1991) writes:

> Those Muslims who interpreted their faith more esoterically or mystically, saw nothing wrong in adapting Islam to the local Indian environment, its mores and traditions, its languages and symbols. Indeed, it is precisely the indigenization of the faith that was instrumental in spreading, so successfully, fundamental Islamic precepts among the local populations. As part of this process, concepts are 'Indianized' or 'indigenized' and presented in terms that would be familiar and palatable to Indian audiences. (Asani 1991: 221)

However, to understand that there was a total transformation which came about within a short period of time would be a mistake because of the dialectical relationship between change and continuity. In the beginning, there was a conscious effort to keep the *masnavī* true to the Persian model of the genre. As a result, even at a later date some features were preserved and retained as opposed to some that were disregarded, redesigned or assimilated.

As one proceeds to take a closer look at the Indo-Sufi *masnavī* literature in general, the following important question arises. What aspects of the Persian *masnavī* tradition have been retained and how does the Indo-Sufi *masnavī* incorporate elements from Indic literature?

Establishing as models the first four of the earliest Indo-Sufi *masnavīs*, i.e. the *Cāndāyan* of Daud (1379), *Mṛgāvatī* of Kutuban (1503), *Padmāvat* of Jayasi (1547), and *Madhumālatī* of Manjhan (1545) as examples, in this chapter I discuss some of the general formal or structural features of Indo-Sufi *masnavī* literature, map the thematic features and the aesthetics of this genre, and discuss the prosody, with emphasis on the metrical structure of *Cāndāyan*.

As the Indo-Sufi *masnavī* genre evolved into an independent poetic form different in flavour from the original Persian model, many features that were traditional to the Persian *masnavī* were retained, some were transformed, and many new features were borrowed from indigenous literary traditions.

A careful study of the Indo-Sufi *masnavī* literature makes it quite clear that an overriding number of the *masnavī* compositions share certain features which are common to all the romances. These features can, in turn, be divided into two distinct categories. First, the formal or the structural properties of the Indo-Sufi *masnavī* texts and, secondly, the thematic characteristics which essentially endow the genre with its identifying features. By 'formal structure' I mean the set pattern typical of the *masnavī* genre that dictates how the text is laid out.

Before we begin to discuss the formal properties let us take a moment to familiarize ourselves with the general storylines and the sources of inspiration for the *masnavīs*. *Cāndāyan*, as discussed in some detail in Chapter 2, is based on the locally popular folk narrative *Canainī* or *Cāndā-Lorik*. This oral tradition is alive in performance today. Interestingly, the story has many regional variations and is told in many differing dialects of what is generally accepted as the Awadhī language.[1]

Padmāvat is based on historical events. According to Jindal:

> Unlike his predecessors, Jayasi has not based the story of his *Padmāvat* on an imaginary plot. The story centres around the historical fact of the siege of Chittore in AD 1290, with some modifications to suit the purpose of the narrative. Ratansen, the then king of Mewar has been mentioned as the hero, instead of Bhīmsen who was on the throne when the episode happened. The journey to Ceylon to win Padmāvatī is also a figment of the poet's imagination. All else is strictly true. There is so much of historical truth in the book that F.E. Keay has been misled into describing Jayasi as a bardic chronicler of his times. (Jindal 1993: 41)[2]

Although *Cāndāyan* is the earliest Indo-Sufi *masnavī* we have thus far, and subsequent *masnavīs* seem to be modelled in many respects on it, by far the best known work of this genre is Malik Muhammad Jayasi's

Padmāvat composed in 1540. Many scholars such as Charlotte Vaudeville, M. Gupta, and Rajnath Sharma have published extensive work on this later *masnavī*.

It was believed until recently that the stories of *Mṛgāvatī* and *Madhumālatī* are essentially imaginary; they incorporate a number of magical occurrences such as humans taking animal forms; some of the elements are essentially borrowed from Hindu mythology. However, recent research materials confirm that inspiration for *Mṛgāvatī* (composed in 1503 by poet Kutuban in the reign of Hussain Shah Sharqi of Bengal) comes from a folktale that can be traced back to the Jaina texts. According to the legend, Mṛgāvatī was the wife of Rājā Śatanīka who was a contemporary of Mahavira. In Jaina Mahāyāna texts, Mṛgāvatī is one of sixteen chaste women. Her name and story are also mentioned in the Jaina Mahāyāna text, in *Suman-Manoraha* episode.[3]

The story of *Madhumālatī* of Manjhan develops along lines similar to *Mṛgāvatī*. Prince Manohar is carried in his sleep by the nymphs to the bed chamber of Madhumālatī. Upon waking, both fall in love with each other. However, the nymphs transport the prince back to his kingdom. This story, like the other *masnavīs*, is also about the quest of lovers and about the various difficulties they encounter in their endeavour to find each other.

Let us now examine the specific formal or structural features of Indo-Sufi *masnavī* and analyse which of these derive from Persian traditions and which are borrowed from the Indian literary tradition.

Indo-Sufi *masnavī* are composed in the local vernacular. The most obvious feature common to all Indo-Sufi *masnavīs* is that the entire text is a unified whole and is not divided into different cantos or *sargas*. In contrast to the Indian *mahākāvya* or epic tradition, where the story is divided into more than eight sections or *sargas*, no such division is required in the Persian *masnavī* tradition. A new episode or digression within the framework of the larger story may be introduced by a title phrase or sentence, often in prose form. Interestingly, this particular feature is maintained only in *Cāndāyan*. In *Cāndāyan*, each of the *kaḍvaks* is initially announced by an introductory phrase or sentence in Persian prose. Subsequent composition such as *Mṛgāvatī*, *Padmāvat*, and *Madhumālatī* do not have introductory phrases between the *kaḍvaks*.

This leads us to the next noteworthy feature. The Persian *masnavī* may maintain a single meter throughout the entire composition. Following the Persian pattern, and unlike the Indian *mahākāvya*, the text of the Indo-Sufi *masnavī* also continues in the same meter throughout. The poet used this freedom and selected the meter most suitable for the mood or tempo of their story. Therefore, in the above respect also, the Indo-Sufi *masnavī* seems to follow the pattern established by the Persian tradition, because according to the Indian *mahākāvya* tradition, the meter of an epic may differ from *sarga* to *sarga*.[4] In fact, at the very end of a given *sarga* a new meter can be introduced and the following *sarga* is then composed in this newly introduced meter. This way a poet could show his craftsmanship by composing in a variety of poetic meters.

The introduction of a new meter was perhaps meant to accomplish two goals. It helps to break the monotony of the narrative in addition to giving the poet an opportunity to show off his expertise in more than one meter, as mentioned above. It is important to note, at this point, that the Apabhraṁśa epic narratives do not strictly observe the rules laid down for the Sanskrit *mahākāvyas*; instead of dividing the epic into clearly marked *sargas*, the narrative is somewhat fused together. Kutuban acknowledges that in his *Mṛgāvatī* he follows the model of the *Apabhraṁśa chanda* (Batra 1993: 477).

Each new episode in the Persian *masnavī* genre is introduced by a title before that particular episode. Within its general framework, a *masnavī* may contain several sections, as digressions or anecdotes, provided that the main storyline is sustained throughout the entire composition. Each of these digressions may contain a completely independent story, or an anecdote, to expound a certain didactic lesson. Each of these sections has its own subtitle, often in prose, indicating the beginning of a particular episode. In a way, the title or introductory phrase is as characteristic of the Persian *masnavī* literature as the *sarga* is to Indian classical literature. In the case of the Persian *masnavī*, these digressions are mostly instrumental in clarifying a certain point or issue raised in the main body of the story. For example, in Rumi's *masnavī*, frequent digressions are employed to explain a complicated issue that requires an explanation or comment, and then the story comes back to where it left off. It is fascinating to observe that in the evolution of the Indo-Sufi *masnavī*, the mannerism of announcing the next episode by means of a rubric or introductory phrase, usually written out in red ink, did not survive beyond the very first Indo-Sufi *masnavī, Cāndāyan*.

A classic example of a frame story which incorporates many stories within its main narrative is *The Arabian Nights*, in which principal stories sometimes incorporate several minor anecdotes. Digressions may also be used as a means to provide background information on a new character or to present justification for an action or decision. On the surface, the actions of a character may appear illogical or unwise to the outsider, but have great wisdom behind them. The complexity of the subject matter more or less mandates the need to explain the course of action at some length. This necessitates the creation of short digressions. At this point it is best to point out that *The Arabian Nights* is by no means a particular example of the use of digression.

As a structural feature, similar to the *sarga* or canto, digression breaks the routine and relieves the monotony of the narrative and often provides comic relief or some other contrasting emotion in an otherwise lengthy or serious discourse. According to Shyam Manohar Pandey,

> In the Persian *masnavī* tradition, rubrics are provided for each single episode. Nizami, Amir Khusrau, Jami, and Faizi have given rubrics introducing the following episodes in their *masnavīs*. In the original manuscripts of the early Indo-Sufi *masnavīs*, these rubrics are in the Persian language. Therefore it seems that the Sufi poets have followed the tradition of the Persian *masnavīs* in the above respect. (Pandey 1961: 261)

The next noteworthy formal feature of an Indo-Sufi *masnavī* is that it always opens with verses offering praise to God.[5] At first glance, it is not difficult to link this feature to the original *masnavī* tradition of Persia. Traditionally, a Persian *masnavī* also begins with a few opening devotional couplets written in praise of God. This section of the composition is called the *hamd* in the Persian *masnavī* tradition. *Hamd* in Arabic means praise exclusively of God. In the Indo-Sufi *masnavīs* the *hamd* is maintained, although it gets very much shortened. The five-page-long *hamd* section in the *masnavī* of Amir Khusrau, *Duwal Rani Khazir Khan*, opens as follows:

> S'ar-e nāmah beh nām-e ān Khodāvand
> Keh delhā rā beh khubān dād payvand
> Ze eshq ārāst lowh-e āb o gel rā
> bedān jān zendagī bakhshīd del rā (Nizami 1988: 7).

> I begin the composition in the name of that God
> Who grafted hearts to beauty,
> Who adorned the tablet of water and clay with
> the life that makes the heart throb.

The opening lines from the first stanza or *kaḍvak* of the *hamd* section from *Cāndāyan* follows:

> पहले गाउं सिरजन हारू।
> जिनि सिरज्या यह देस दयारू।। (M. Gupta 1967: 1)

First of all, I sing of the Creator
Who (has) created this region and place.

In the first *kaḍvak* Maulana Daud praises God who created the universe (literally region and place), the constellations, the sun, the moon, and the stars in the sky. In the second *kaḍvak* he praises God for creating the earth in nine parts, the ocean and the pearls, the gems, and the sea animals which are a treasure to mankind. In the third *kaḍvak* he praises the Creator for creating the different animals roaming the earth, fire, gold, and plants with healing qualities. Surprisingly, in His vast creation, there is no place beyond His presence. The fourth stanza praises God for creating man and for creating nourishing foods for him and the various plants and animals. In the fifth stanza, Daud wonders how God puts musk in the body of the deer who wanders from one wilderness to another, looking for that which is within.

This last portion of the *hamd* section of *Cāndāyan* is extremely significant in terms of the expression of Sufi beliefs. In one single stanza at the very beginning of the epic, with amazing ingenuity, the author has already introduced the fundamentals of Sufi philosophy, i.e. the relationship of the soul with the Maker. In fact, in the lines, 'How God puts the musk in the body of the deer who wildly wanders from jungle to jungle, looking for that which is within' the gist of the entire poem is encapsulated. The image of the restless deer looking for musk is merely a familiar, pretty picture. Daud is using the deer as an analogue of the human soul caught within the trappings of material form. Form or body essential for formal existence is tangible, ephemeral, and hence perpetually vulnerable. The very picture of the lovely deer panting and yet bounding about looking for the musk which is within its own being arouses compassion in the reader or listener.

Musk, in turn, is a symbol of God, intangible and yet totally engaging, inaccessible and yet, as the Koran says, closer to man than his jugular vein. Maulana Daud is introducing the idea that God is within man. A man should look within himself for eternal happiness and contentment instead of searching for them outside. However, it is quite clear that for a human being to understand this wisdom and abandon his quest in the material world is going to be just as difficult as explaining to the deer not to look for the musk all around him because it is in him already.

The Sufis often compare the soul, which restlessly seeks God, to a mirror. The reflection is an inseparable part of the mirror but the mirror does not know this. According to Annemarie Schimmel:

One of the most fascinating objects in religious history is the mirror, from ancient times an object sacred to the Japanese goddess Amaterasu. Mirrors were made of steel and had to be polished carefully so that they could reflect persons or objects. The Koranic saying 'What they were earning was overshadowing their hearts' could easily be applied to the mirror of the heart that was covered by the rust of blameworthy actions and was thus no longer capable of reflecting the Divine light. This theme was to become a favourite with the Sufis, who tried (and continue to try) to instruct the disciple in how to polish this mirror by constant recollection of God lest any dust, rust, or verdigris of evil actions or thoughts be collected on it. (Schimmel 1994: 31)

A total of five stanzas in *Cāndāyan's* are dedicated to the *hamd*. In comparison, in Jayasi's *Padmāvat*, the *hamd* section comprises ten *kaḍvaks*; *Madhumālatī* and *Mṛgāvatī* both take three. The *hamd* sections described above however, seem much shorter when compared with the 59 couplets of the *hamd* section in *Duwal Rani Khazir Khan* of Amir Khusrau (Nizami 1988: 1–5). From the above survey, it may also be concluded that there is no set number of couplets or stanzas required for the *hamd* section of an Indo-Sufi *masnavī*.

In an Indo-Sufi m*asnavī* the *hamd* section is invariably followed by a panegyric couplet in honour of the Prophet. The section so introduced is called the *nāt*. Sometimes the Prophet's legendary journey to the heavens is described; sometimes honorific mention of his companions follows. In *Cāndāyan*, the *nāt* section comprises of only one *kaḍvak*. The *kaḍvak* following the *nāt kaḍvak* is composed in honour of the four companions of the Prophet. The following are the first two lines of the *nāt* section from *Cāndāyan*.

पुरिषु येकु सिरसजि उजियारा।
नाउ महंमदु जगतु पियारा।। (M. Gupta 1967: 6)

The Light, created a man,
Muhammad by name, dear to the world.[6]

In *Mṛgāvatī*, as well as in *Padmāvat*, the above pattern is observed. In other words, only one stanza is dedicated to the *nāt* section. In *Madhumālatī*, however, the seventh and the eighth *kaḍvaks* make up the *nāt* section followed by the ninth in praise of the four friends of the Prophet. Additionally, it may be observed that there is no fixed number of stanzas for the *nāt* section. The *nāt* section is important for another reason. If it mentions the four Caliphs, our guess would be that the author is of the Sunnī persuasion. If the blessing of the five members of the Prophet's family, the twelve imāms, or the fourteen innocent ones were also to be evoked, the *nāt* section would then give the reader a sign of the poet's Shia persuasion.

After praising God and the Prophet and his companions, the author of an Indo-Sufi *masnavī* pays his respects to the reigning king and then to his own pīr. For example, in *Cāndāyan*, Mulla Daud has composed one *kaḍvak* for each of the above topics. In the eighth *kaḍvak* Maulana Daud praises the *Shah-i-waqt*, Firoz Shah Tughlaq. In the ninth stanza he mentions his own Pīr, Shaikh Zainuddin.

साहि पेरोज ढीली बड राजा।
छात पाट औ ते पए छाजा।। (M. Gupta 1967: 8)

King Firoz is the great ruler of Delhi.
The (royal) parasol and the throne are befitting to him alone.

सेष पंथु हौ पथि लावा।
धरम पंथु जिह पापु गवावा।। (M. Gupta 1967: 9)

Shaikh Zainuddin brought me to the (true) path,
The path of virtue, so that (my) sin(s) may be depleted.

According to Pathak, to have a spiritual pīr is of pivotal importance for a follower who walks the Sufi path of love. The guru's commands are simply beyond question. The disciple hangs on to every single word of the guru (Pathak 1978: 55). The premise is that if you have somebody with you who has already been to your chosen destination, it is easier because you have a guide who is already experienced. For the Sufis, the guru or the spiritual preceptor is that guide.

Elaborating on the above theme, in the last but one *kaḍvak* (#425) of *Mṛgāvatī*, Kutuban says to the reader that this *masnavī* must be read with the help of a teacher who is already initiated, because, by the time an unguided layman can figure out the intricate meaning, 'dusk would have already fallen'. The relationship of the teacher and the disciple is known as *pīrī-murīdī*. Pinto has studied this phenomenon in Sufi practice from a sociological perspective (Pinto 1995).

Coming back to the formal characteristics of *Cāndāyan*, in the 10th through the 17th *kaḍvaks* the author praises his patron Khan-i-Jahan and a supporter, Malik Mubarak, who is a brave and generous courtier. Here is what Daud writes about Khan-i-Jahan:

खानजहां घरि जुग जुग षानी।
अजि नागरु बुधिवंतु बिनानी।। (M. Gupta 1967: 10)

Khan-i-Jahan belongs to the Khan family, famous from past ages.
He is extremely sophisticated, wise, and well-established.

In the *Mṛgāvatī*, the sixth stanza is dedicated to the pīr of the author, but the following four stanzas praise the *shah-i-waqt*, the current ruler, Hussain Shah. In *Padmāvat*, after the *hamd* and *nāt* sections, Malik Muhammad Jayasi first praises Sher Shah, the Sultan of Delhi, for five *kaḍvaks*, then proceeds to praise his spiritual guide and his lineage for three more. Similarly, in *Madhumālatī*, Manjhan first praises the reigning king Salim in four *kaḍvaks* and his spiritual Pīr Shaikh Ghaus Muhammad in seven. Then he praises his patron.

From the above survey, the observation can be made that the *hamd* and the *nāt* sections are important formal features of Indo-Sufi *masnavī* literature. The *nāt* section usually follows the opening section of *hamd*, which is always placed at the beginning of the text. Praise of the reigning king, the spiritual pīr, and the patron, and providing the time-frame, the poets own introduction, and sometimes the justification for writing are also significant formal features. However, sometimes their sequence can be altered: the praise of the pīr may be placed either before or after the praise of the *shah-i-waqt*. Also, the number of stanzas to be allocated to each of the above formal features is flexible.

The most significant formal feature of Indo-Sufi *masnavī* literature, from the historical point of view, is the date of composition. After fulfilling the formalities of acknowledgements, the author states the date of his composition and introduces himself. Sometimes this is followed by the justification for writing, commonly known as the *arz-i-musannif* or author's statement. The following couplet, providing the time the composition of *Cāndāyan* was compiled, comes from its 17th *kaḍvak*.

बरस सात सै होये इक्यासी।
तिहि याह कबि सरसे उभासी।। (M. Gupta 1967: 17)

It was the year 781 (Hijri) when this poet recited this interesting (composition).

Although the information regarding the date of a composition is an integral part of that composition, problems of dating literary works still arise. The root of this problem is the legibility of the script. Sometimes the formation of letter *alif* and *alif lām* together or the formation of two dots or *nuqtās* together in the manner of a dash make it difficult to determine the correct reading. Sometimes the contemporary pronunciation of certain key words contributes to the problem. For instance, in some dialects of Awadhī, in the Awadhī-speaking areas of modern Uttar

Pradesh, Madhya Pradesh, and Bihar, the word for a hundred, *sau*, was pronounced and written, for many centuries, as *sai*, *saya*, *sāu* or *se*. This practice, interestingly, still prevails in many areas of Uttar Pradesh and is attested by written as well as spoken language samples. Similar problems often raise doubts in determining the accurate date of a given composition. *Padmāvat* is a good example. In Mataprasad Gupta's edition (1963: 1–5), the question of the dating of *Padmāvat* is discussed over four pages.

Discussing the problems stemming from the writing systems, Ali Asani in his *Būjh Niranjan* writes:

> The texts of the *Būjh Niranjan* employ three scripts: the Perso-Arabic, the Khojki, and the Gujrati. Of the three, the Perso-Arabic and the Khojki present a complex set of problems during the perusal of the text. For a variety of reasons that will be discussed below, these two scripts fail to record fully and precisely the complete range of vowels and consonants of an Indian language. Consequently, readers often have to rely on personal judgement in determining the correct reading of a particular word. For instance, the Perso-Arabic script, though it possesses the technical means to record short vowels, normally requires readers to supply these vowels as they read the text. Thus, the word 'pvṭ' may be read as pata, pita, puta, pati, patu, piti, pitu, or putu. This hypothetical example illustrates well the nature of the problems that may arise while ascertaining the reading of texts written in the two scripts. However, the modern configurations of the Perso-Arabic script (its Urdu and Sindhi versions) as well as Khojki have been so refined and standardized that, on the whole, they are better able to record a text such as the *Būjh Niranajan*, perhaps not so adequately as the traditional Devanagari-based scripts. But this was not the case with the medieval prototypes of the two scripts which were characterized by imperfection of form and inconsistency of usage. Consequently, script-related problems can become particularly serious during the reconstruction of a medieval text such as the *Būjh Niranjan*, which often makes use of little-known and archaic grammatical forms and vocabulary. (Asani 1991: 47)

Asani goes on to explain that the manuscripts of medieval literature which are recorded in the Devanagari-based scripts are products of more recent times and that the readings of the editions printed in the present century are not completely reliable. Extensive manuscript work on these texts by scholars completely at ease with Perso-Arabic and Devanagari-based writing systems is required, as well as knowledge of the meanings of words that have fallen out of usage.

Should controversy arise regarding the date of a particular text, additional information from the formal features of a *masnavī*, such as the name of the reigning sultan, the name of the pīr, the patron's name, and the native place of the author, help a great deal in resolving the problem.

To determine if the above-described formal features of the Indo-Sufi *masnavī* are traditionally Persian in nature or are borrowed from Indian literature, let us examine the elements in the *Laila-Majnūn* of Nizami of Ganja (d. 1209). Nizami was a powerful poet and a great many poets, including Amir Khusrau, during and after his time were deeply influenced by him. In the *Masnavī-i-Laila-Majnūn*, Nizami first praises God and the Prophet. Then he describes the Prophet's journey to the heavens, the *merāj*.

Cāndāyan does not have the portion called *merāj*. A contemporary poet, Abdul Quddus Gangohi, planned to write a Persian version of *Cāndāyan*. This Persian version was well underway when Sultan Bahlol had to fight Sultan Hussain. In this struggle, the bulk of the manuscript was destroyed. A few couplets have been found preserved in writing which give us an idea of his plan:

> Hazrat Kutubi Abdul Quddus Gangohi planned presently to make a Persian version of the Hindawi manuscript of *Cāndāyan* and after the description of the praise of God and the praise of the Prophet, he wanted to write something about the journey of the Prophet to the heavens because in *Cāndāyan*, the description of *Meraj* (the legendary journey of Prophet to the heavens) is not there. (V. Prasad 1962: 4)

This makes one wonder whether because of the lack of the *merāj* section, among the more conservative elites of the times, *Cāndāyan* was regarded as somewhat deficient and efforts were being made to make up for this in the Persian version of *Cāndāyan*.

The next feature common to the Persian and the Indo-Sufi *masnavī* is the statement of purpose. For instance, in one of the Indo-Sufi *masnavīs*, after mentioning his patron who commissioned the *masnavī*, the author proceeds to inform us that the reason for writing it is to provide a guideline for appropriate conduct for his son. Rumi on numerous occasions states that the purpose of his *Masnavī* is to provide guidance for spiritual enlightenment. Therefore, it seems that in most Indo-Sufi *masnavī* literature, the formal properties of the Persian *masnavī* are observed.

Based on the above observation, some scholars of Hindi literature have concluded that in the course of studying the Indo-Sufi *masnavīs*, time and again, we are faced with features that have been preserved from the Persian *masnavī* tradition. Hindi scholars (R.P. Mishra 1982:

18, Mishra and Pandey 1967: 60) support the theory of Ram Chandra Shukla that the Indo-Sufi allegorical romances are basically, in terms of their formal structure, modelled after the Persian *masnavīs* (Gulati 1979: 25).

Is the above information sufficient to conclude that Indo-Islamic *masnavī* literature, in terms of its formal features, exclusively followed the Persian model? It should be kept in mind that Indian vernacular poetry as well as folk poetry of Jainas also follows a similar pattern. For example, Puṣpadanta's *Mahāpurāṇa*, and Svayambhu's *Pauma-cariyam* do begin with devotional poetry honouring the *Jina*. Often this feature is followed by the praise of Saraswati; then the reigning king is recognized. The poet then introduces himself and the patron is mentioned and sometimes justification is provided for writing.

In terms of dividing the epic into *sargas*, we have evidence that the rules defined for the composition of the Sanskrit *mahākāvya* were not strictly adhered to by the authors who composed in the Indian vernacular. However, in contemporary popular literature patterns were flourishing which were very similar to the model found in the Indo-Sufi *masnavī* genre.

A digression or a minor story within the main story, or the description of a certain place or an episode, is introduced by a *surkhiyān*, heading or title. This feature was in keeping with the Persian *masnavī* tradition. Sanskrit poetics dictate, that an epic should contain a minimum of eight chapters or *sargas*, but in the Indo-Islamic *masnavīs* this mandate is not observed. In fact no division is constituted and, without breaking into cantos, the story continues uninterrupted. As mentioned, although the Indo-Sufi *masnavī* is not divided into *sargas*, even the feature of the rubric, a sure divider of the various episodes, faded out after the composition of *Cāndāyan* (1379). Once again, we must bear in mind that between the two earliest Indo-Sufi *masnavī* compositions there was an interval of approximately 124 years. It seems that with the passage of time, the Indo-Sufi *masnavī* found itself subject to change.

For precisely the above reasons, many modern scholars such as Batra, Shyam Manohar Pandey, and Mataprasad Gupta, among others, find the study of Indo-Sufi *masnavī* literature fascinating. The available literary treasure offers the scholar a rare glimpse of life frozen in time. It is interesting not only from the point of view of linguistics, but also in its socio-cultural aspects. For example, when the Sufi immigrants who were well versed in the Persian literary tradition wished to send their message to the common people of their region, they adopted the local language as well as the common or folk poetic meters.

The study of the metrical patterns of the early Indo-Sufi literature is also interesting. Although the Indo-Sufi poets had adopted many indigenous literary features, they were still recording their compositions in the Perso-Arabic script which is partial to the syllabic system, as opposed to the alphabetic writing system of the Devanagari script. In addition, the authors were used to composing in couplets. When they adopted the *caupāī* meter of the Awadhi language, they considered the first two rhyming feet of the meter as a complete unit. As a result, it is quite evident that many formal features of the Persian *masnavī* tradition and the features of the vernacular Indic literature do conflate in the early Indo-Sufi *masnavī* literature. This issue will be discussed further in the section on prosody at the end of this chapter.

Thematic Features

In combination with the formal characteristics, thematic features give a unique identity to the Indo-Sufi *masnavīs*. The following features, again, are common to a large majority of them.

Amir Khusrau (d. 1325), who wrote *masnavīs* in India in Persian, cast his long-lasting influence on the Indo-Sufi poets of the coming generations, including Maulana Daud and Malik Muhammad Jayasi.[7] Amir Khusrau is considered to be responsible for introducing a number of new Indic features, such as the description of the Indian rituals and landscapes, into his own *masnavīs*. He encouraged and established precedents for the practice of adopting and improvising literary features of the Indic tradition. Although Amir Khusrau's *masnavīs* were composed in Persian, most scholars consider him to have been well versed in many other languages including Hindawi, Arabic, and Turkish (Mishra and Pandey 1967: 37). His Hindawi compositions were perhaps stepping stones for the authors of the Indo-Sufi *masnavīs* for their choice of language. Regrettably, a considerable volume of his very valuable Hindawi writings have been lost, even though a variety of compositions have survived. Among these, his riddles and *qawwali* compositions in Hindawi are worthy of special mention.

A detailed study on the influence of Amir Khusrau's *masnavīs* on future writers is much needed. Chronologically, Amir Khusrau's *masnavīs* are a landmark in the history of Indian literature. Even though all of them are written in Persian in 'rhyming doublets', as Browne (1902: 452) puts it, these are essentially the forerunners of the Indo-Sufi *masnavī* literature composed just half a century after his death.

It is said that Khusrau was deeply influenced by the Persian poet Nizami Ganjavi (d. 1209). Khusrau designed his own *Khamsa* (set of five *masnavīs*) on the model of Nizami's *Khamsa*. Nizami's five *masnavīs* are: *Khusrau and Śīrīn*, *Lailā-Majnūn*, *Makhzan ul-Asrār*, *Haft Paikar*, and *Eskandar-Nāma*.[8] Amir Khusrau was not the only poet to follow Nizam's example. In his own country, Persia, for example, Khāje of Kirman (1281–1352) also composed a set of five *masnavīs* (S.M. Pandey 1968: 189). Nevertheless, Amir Khusrau had introduced many non-Persian features in his *masnavī* compositions. These new features were later canonized and used as a blueprint by *masnavī* writers in India and, in the long run, they played a significant role in shaping the features which gradually became common to most Indo-Sufi *masnavī* compositions.

An analytical glance at the indigenous elements introduced by Khusrau is essential at this point because the Sufi poets did not simply imitate Khusrau. The changes Khusrau introduced were used by writers of the following generations not only as a springboard to also introduce various innovations, but also as a license to continue to incorporate additional indigenous elements.

Using the literary features already present in the genre as the basis for digressions and spin-offs,[9] and building on the existing structures using their own creative imagination, the Sufi poets of India created wonderful narratives. Even if there was an initial effort to keep the *masnavī* true to the original model, there was also an environment that was conducive to change. Consequently, a gradual indigenization process took place. This process of introducing and implementing changes, adopting local features and improvising on them, and/or changing them to suit a purpose, continued and prospered simultaneously as the volume of Indo-Sufi *masnavī* literature expanded and flourished.

A good example of this is the following feature found only in Indo-Sufi *masnavīs*. In the *masnavīs* of Nizami and Khusrau, the heroine often is already a married woman. According to Pandey (1968: 195), this accounts for the greater suffering of the hero of the Persian *masnavī* when compared with the hero of the Indo-Sufi *masnavī*. Contrary to the above and in conformity with Indian tradition, the heroine of the Indo-Sufi *masnavī* is always a virgin (see Chapter 6 for details).

As the practice of adaptation continued, numerous changes occurred within the standard framework of the storyline of Indo-Sufi *masnavī* literature so that the individual stories, despite their basic similarities, began to be interesting and sufficiently different from each other. A couple of general points, once again, should be made clear at this juncture. In addition to the fact that the Indo-Sufi *masnavī* in Awadhī is defined by its subject matter rather than by any specific metrical considerations, most Indo-Sufi *masnavīs* have a more or less standard storyline which alters rather little from composition to composition. Mishra and Pandey write:

> From the point of view of organizing the storyline, the Sufi love narratives are quite similar to each other. The story often opens with the description of the birth of the hero and the heroine. In their youth, they are introduced to each other by an agent. This is followed by the hero leaving home in quest of the heroine. The second part of the narrative addresses the problems the hero faces in his quest. In the last third of the composition, the hero and the heroine are united and the hero returns home. (Mishra and Pandey 1967: 57)

Ram Prasad Mishra agrees.

> The Sufi epics and episodes of Hindi, from the Chandaayan (fourteenth century) to the Indraawati (eighteenth century), possess a unique sameliness of plot, meter, style, and message. All deal with a common plot. The hero comes to know about the matchless beauty and grace of the heroine, leaves all the worldly things and goes in her search, and after great difficulties reaches the destination, and, here too, faces many obstacles, but ultimately gets the heroine, and, thus, the plot, in general, bears the note of a comedy, as in the Madhumaalti of Manjhan. (Mishra 1982: 34)

For approximately 200 years before Amir Khusrau, a number of writers in India were writing in Persian. The court language was Persian for many years before and after Khusrau. Moreover, the description of Persian landscapes, styles of clothing, and customs was considered to be more prestigious than the portrayal of Indian scenery and indigenous social life. It is interesting to notice that although this trend changed in the Indo-Sufi *masnavī* tradition, it continued to prosper in India in the Urdu classical literary forms almost to the turn of the twentieth century. Indian poets, even those who had never been to Persia, sang of *Jam-i-Jam* (the legendary drinking cup of the Persian king Jamshid) and *band-i-qabā* (ribbon of a long robe); the beauty of the *sarv* tree and *gul-i-lala* (tulip); the scent of *sunbul* (hyacinth) and the song of the *bulbul* (nightingale); the wisdom of the *hudhud* (hoopoe) and the tenacity of the *sīmurgh* (a fabulous bird)—none of which are typical of India. The Urdu ghazal was the prime example of this practice in later centuries.[10]

Amir Khusrau is an important figure in the history of Indian literature because he was the first to describe Indian scenes, rituals, and landscapes with appreciation in the Persian language. He was fascinated with the concept of a Hindu married woman (*suhāgin*). Khusrau writes in a famous couplet, 'One must learn how to love from a Hindu woman. Not only does she love her man when he is living but, even in his death, she does not abandon him.' Also consider the following phrases taken from some of Khusrau's compositions: '*Khusrau rain suhāg kī, so main jāgī pī ke sang*' (Khusrau says, 'that lucky night of union, I stayed awake with (my) love') and '*Khusrau Nijām ke bali bali jaiye, mohe suhāgan kīnhīn, mose nainā milāi ke*' ('Khusrau lays down his life for Nijam [Nizamuddin Aulia, the spiritual preceptor of Amir Khusrau] who has put me in a state of bliss by throwing me a glance').[11]

Amir Khusrau initiated the description of intercourse between lovers in *Khusrau-Śīrīn*. This *masnavī*, composed in Persian meters and language, followed the Persian tradition of the *masnavī* genre in all other respects. According to Shyam Manohar Pandey,

> The description of sexual intercourse is not a part of the Persian *masnavī* tradition. Khusrau adopted this from the Indic literary tradition. Following his example, in many of the subsequent Indo-Sufi *masnavīs*, very well organized *saṁbhoga* (sexual intercourse) sections can be observed. (Pandey 1968: 197–8)

Although the Persian Poet Jami[12] is said to have been impressed with Khusrau, when Khusrau introduced the Indian literary feature of describing *saṁbhoga* in his *masnavī*, Jami, interestingly, did not adopt it. Here is what Pandey has to say:

> There is another very clear difference between Nizami and Amir Khusrau. Amir Khusrau has described *saṁbhoga* in his *masnavī Śīrīn-Khusrau*. Describing the episode of Khusrau and Śīrīn, Amir Khusrau writes that when Khusrau was intoxicated, he left all the other beauties and went away to a private place in order to rest and enjoy. (Pandey 1968: 198)

This is followed by a detailed description of passionate kissing, disrobing, abandoning of all control, and being consumed by the fire of love. Pandey continues:

> The Persian *masnavī* literature does not have the description of sexual union as part of the *masnavī* tradition. In the *masnavī Yusuf-Zulaikha* of Jami, Zulaikha is married to the Amir of Egypt. Later she is married to Yusuf but the non-Indian Jami did not describe the union of the two in terms of sexual intercourse. Amir Khusrau adopted this practice following the example of the Indian literary tradition. (Ibid: 198)

Unlike Jami, Abu al-Faiz Faizi, the court poet of Akbar and eldest brother of Abul Fazl, did incorporate a description of love and union in his *masnavī, Nala-Daman* (the story of King Nala and Damayantī from the *Mahābhārata*).

In addition to the above, in his *masnavī, Lailā-Majnūn*, Amir Khusrau altered the story by having Qais marry a woman, other than Laila. This had a long-lasting effect on Indo-Sufi *masnavī* literature because many of the heroes of the Indo-Sufi *masnavīs*, such as Lorik and Ratansen, are married men.

The thematic features of Indo-Sufi *masnavī* literature are shaped by two general sources of inspiration. According to Pathak and Chandel (1976: 106–7), one source is the original, indigenous folklore and the other is the poet's own imagination (Pathak 1978: 358). For example, of the two 'snakebite' episodes in *Cāndāyan*, one is borrowed from folklore and the other has been added by Daud (Mataprasad Gupta 1967: 35).

Both the folk tradition and the author's talent for telling a tale contribute to the making of the textual features of the Indo-Sufi *masnavīs*. *Cāndāyan*, as we know, is the first available Indo-Sufi composition and served as a model for later compositions. It is important to understand that when certain highlights from the storyline of *Cāndāyan* were adopted and elaborated upon many times in later *masnavīs*, only then did these textual features come to collectively form the identifying features of the Indo-Sufi *masnavī* literature as a whole. In other words, in the early *masnavīs* composed after *Cāndāyan*, many of the essential features from *Cāndāyan* were adopted and others were added. In time these features were canonized and incorporated into the *masnavīs* that came still later.

Let us now follow the storyline of *Cāndāyan* to help establish and discuss the textual features that are common in the Indo-Sufi *masnavī* genre. The features described below are common to Indo-Sufi *masnavīs* in the sense that they are found in the text of the majority of the *masnavīs* mentioned in our list (Chapter 1).

The romance begins with the description of Govar, the place where the heroine Cāndā was born in the royal household. The luxurious royal palace, the gorgeous gardens, the wonderful wares in the Govar market, and the great diversity of people of Govar make it an enviable place.

> अगरु चंदन उषंटना अछइ सुहाई बासु।
> देवलोक अस भाषहिं म कहुं आहि कबलासु।। (M. Gupta 1967: 30)

> Incense, sandalwood and perfumed lotions
> (in Govar) always keep the air fragrant.
> (This confuses) the gods in the heavens.
> (Amazed they) say: Is this Kailāśa (lord Śiva's abode)!

The description of the environment in which the story takes place is a standard feature of Sufi narratives. The two important points that should be noted here are that, first, the story of *Cāndāyan* was inspired by the folktale of *Canainī*, also known as *Loriki*, and, second, the poet is describing scenes which are familiar to the local people. In fact, for the *masnavīs* of subsequent generations such as *Mṛgāvatī, Padmāvat, Madhumālatī*, and *Citrāvalī* the plot was inspired by indigenous literature or folklore and the description of the places and the landscape is Indian.

Cāndā, the incomparable beauty, is born under the most auspicious stars. She grows up to be a woman of beauty and accomplishment, hence belongs in the first of four traditional classes of women (McGregor 1993: 599).[13] The tales of her loveliness spread far and wide and her father begins to receive many marriage proposals for her, even when she is only twelve months old. To betrothe a girl child in marriage this early was an old Indian custom, called *bālvivāh*:

बरहे मांस देसि गई बाता।
धौर समंद माबर गुजराता।। (M. Gupta 1967: 34)

(With)in the twelfth month (or within twelve months) the information (about Cāndā's beauty and virtue) spread (all the way) to the bordering ports (literally the ocean doors), the Malabar coast and to the Gujrat region.

When Cāndā was four years old, one of the many proposals was accepted, on the grounds that the almanacs of the future bride and the groom matched favourably. This feature comes from local social customs. Although the Iranian and Indian love affair with the science of astrology (*jyotiṣa/nujūm*) is well documented from ancient times, a Muslim marriage may not be arranged or cancelled on the basis of astrological signs. Cāndā's father says the following words to the astrologer:

तोर कहा हउं कैसे मेटहुं सुनि कइ रहउं लजाइ।
गनत रासि जनि भूलहि पाछे होइ पछिताइ।। (M. Gupta 1967: 37)

How can I disregard your words?
I am embarrassed even as I hear them (myself);
However, (keep this in mind that) if mistakes are made in calculating the signs of the zodiac, one has regrets later.

Unlike a Muslim marriage, a Hindu marriage is rarely finalized before the horoscope (*janma patrī*) of the bride and the groom are studied. Not just marriage, but at each important juncture in life, a Hindu family consults the stars to find out if the omens are favourable or inauspicious. Later in the story, we observe how adept and skilled Cāndā herself is at reading the signs of the zodiac and making a plan based on astrological configurations.

The contemporary public had deep faith in astrology. People still consult the stars for auspicious and inauspicious signs. In *Cāndāyan*, all important tasks such as marriage, war, and embarking on a journey are preceded by consulting the astrologers. Rūpcand lost the war because the configuration of planets was not favourable for him. Interestingly, modern scholars like Shandilya and M. Gupta are also well versed in the above science. Shahnaz Parveen, in her *Cāndāyan kā Sānskṛtik Adhyayana*, refers to a disagreement between her teacher Shandilya and M. Gupta. Disagreeing with Gupta's interpretation of the astrological signs in his edition of *Cāndāyan*, Shandilya says, 'According to Gupta, the planets of Rāhu and Ghumaketu were in the eighth house. But according to astrology, these two planets are always seven houses away from each other and can never be in the same house. . . .' (Parveen 1985: 50)

After marriage, Cāndā lived in her husband's house for twelve years until she was sixteen. During this time, her husband did not show any interest in her. When Cāndā returns home unhappy, her friends ask her how she liked living with her husband. Upon this, Cāndā, bashfully confides in her friends about the pain she had suffered because of her longing for her husband's love and his complete indifference. This description of her woe is detailed in terms of the entire year, from one season to the next, a device called *bārahmāsā*. The following couplet describes Cāndā's pain during the winter month of Māgha. She says:

माह मासि मोएउं धुंधुवाई।
लागइ सीउ न पिउ बिनु जाई।। (M. Gupta 1967: 51)

The month of Māgha, I spent like a wet wood
(which does not actually burn). It only smokes.
The chill I felt did not dissipate
in the absence of (my) husband.

The *bārahmāsā* is a standard feature of Indo-Sufi *masnavī* literature. Most scholars agree that the *bārahmāsā* of Jayasi's *Padmāvat* where the poet describes the pain of Nāgamatī separated from her husband, Ratansen, is one of the best in Hindi literature

In *Cāndāyan*, the *bārahmāsā* begins in Sāwan, in the rainy season.

In *Padmāvat*, Nāgamatī, the first wife of the hero, describes her tale of woe beginning with the Āsāṛh month of the rainy season. According to Pandey, the *bārahmāsā* was not borrowed from Sanskrit poets, but from folk tradition. He writes:

> The feature of *bārahmāsā* cannot be found in the Sanskrit literature. Vālmiki describes only four seasons in his *Rāmāyaṇa*. In *Ritusaṁhāra*, Kalidasa describes six seasons beginning from summer and culminating in spring. Māgha's *Śiśupālawadha* also describes only six seasons. However, in the contemporary Apabhraṁśa literature, both features were prevalent, i.e., the description of six seasons and the feature of the *bārahmāsā*. (See Abdul Rahman's *Saṁdeś Rāsak.*) Jain poets as well as the Indo-Sufi poets adopted the feature of the *bārahmāsā* from the contemporary folk traditions. (Pandey 1968: 97–104)

Shortly after Cāndā returned to her hometown, a beggar came to Govar. He saw Cāndā on her terrace and 'lost his senses'.

बाजुरु एकु कतहुं हुत आवा।
गोवर फिरइ बिहाऊ गावा।
घर घर भुगुति मांगि लइ खाई।
खिन खिन राजदुवारेहिं जाई।
दिन एक चांद धरौहर ठाढि।
झांकिसि मांथ झरोखइ काढि।
तिहि खिन बाजुर मूंड उचावा
देषि चांद तवारा आवा। (M. Gupta 1967: #54)

A beggar, Bajur, came over to Govar, by way of some other place.
Roaming around, he sang soulful songs.
Working his way from door to door, he begged and ate.
By and by he arrived at the royal gate.
(That) one day, Cāndā was standing at (her) terrace.
To take a peek she put her head out of the window.
Right at that moment, the beggar raised his head.
Seeing Cāndā, he got a fever.

In *Cāndāyan*, loss of the senses recurs twice—first when Lorik sees Cāndā for the first time at a party at her father's house, and when he meets her again at the shrine.

चांद सीसु भगवंतहि नावा।
भा अचेतु मन चेतु गंजावा।। (M. Gupta 1967: 168)

As Cāndā bowed her head to greet the worshipful lord (Lorik), he fell unconscious. His mind lost its wit.

This feature is an extension of a Persian tradition. Before and contemporaneous to Daud, 'fainting' episodes can be found in the Persian compositions of Fariduddin Attar, Shaikh Sadi, and Jami. (For source of inspiration, see Koran 7:143.)[14]

When the beggar Bajur comes to his senses, he leaves town for fear of punishment. After a month of wandering, he arrives in the kingdom of Raja Rūpcand, where, in song, he describes Cāndā's beauty.

चोला चीर पहिरि जउ चाली जानउं जाइ उडाइ।
देखत रूप देवता बिमोहे कत हुतें आछरि आइ।। (M. Gupta 1967: #83)

Wearing her bodice and raiment when she walks,
It seems she is just about to fly.
Looking at her form, the gods are spellbound.
(Confused, they say), Where has this nymph (*apsarā*) come from?

In the Persian literary tradition, the feature where the beauty of the heroine is portrayed in detail is called *sarāpā*, and in Sanskrit *nakhaśikha varṇana*. The description of a woman's beauty is an essential element of the *masnavī* genre. Levy, in his *An Introduction to Persian Literature*, writes:

There is this charming little sketch of Rudaba, who is the heart of Zal:

Within her father's veiled apartment there's a maid whose face is brighter than the sun;
From head to foot she's white as ivory,
her cheek like Heaven, her form a willow's;
Upon her silvern shoulders lie two tresses dark,
their ends like the rings of fetters;
Her mouth a pomegranate blossom, her lip a cherry,
from her silvern breasts grow two pomegranate seeds,
Her eyes are two narcissi in the garden;
her lashes stolen from a raven's wing. (Levy 1969: 72)

William Chittick emphasizes that this was not a mere poetic convention:

According to Sufi teachings women manifest the divine Attributes of Beauty, Mercy, Gentleness, and Kindness in a relatively direct manner within their outward forms. In Rūmī's (1207–73) view, their derivative beauty is the closest thing to True Beauty in the material world. For this very reason, the attraction that their beauty exerts upon a man can be one of the greatest obstacles to his spiritual development. As long as he thinks that a woman's beauty belongs to her, he will be led astray. But once he is able to see her beauty as the reflection of God's Beauty, then his derivative love can be transformed into True Love. (Chittick 1983: 286)

Justifying the literary feature of *sarāpā* or *nakha śikha varṇana*, Pandey writes:

The divine is manifest in beauty and splendour. In *Madhumālatī*, the hero explains to the heroine that the soul is the manifestation of God. The worldly loveliness only reflects the beauty of its Creator. Human beings are endowed with vision so they may enjoy this beauty. To a person with vision, the entire world is resplendent with God's beauty. (S.M. Pandey 1982: 161)

In the *masnavī* genre, as in many of the world's literary genres, love is born when the hero hears the description of the heroine's magnificent beauty. This is also true in the romance tradition of both Europe and Asia. Sometimes it is the heroine who is told of the chivalry of a prince. A parrot, a confidante, a minister, or a traveller acts as the agent. In Shakespeare's *Othello*, Othello explains to the Duke how it was possible for Desdemona to fall in love with him after listening to his tales of adventure and woe:

Her father loved me; oft invited me;
Still questioned me the story of my life
From year to year, the battle, sieges, fortune
That I have passed

In *Padmāvat*, the hero Ratansen learns of the heroine's beauty from a parrot. According to Pandey, in the Indo-Sufi *masnavīs* stories about the virtues of the hero or the heroine, seeing his or her vision in a dream, or seeing his or her portrait can initiate the feelings of love (S.M. Pandey 1982: 224). In *Cāndāyan*, when Bajur tells Rūpcand of Cāndā's beauty, Rūpcand also begins to experience the same fire of love.

तिल संजोग बाजुर सिर कीन्हेउ ओहट भा परु जाइ।
राजा हिए आगि परजारि तिल तिल जरि न बुझाइ।। (M. Gupta 1967: 74)

(The way) Cāndā's mole had struck a blow
on the head of Bajur and he was done in;
The king's heart also began to be burned,
Slowly, little by little, in that inextinguishable fire (of love).

According to Pandey the description of the mole is a feature borrowed from Persian tradition. There is no mention of a mole or beauty spot in either the *Meghadūta* or the *Ṛtusaṁhāra* of Kalidasa. Additionally, neither in *Vāsavadattā* of Subandhu (AD 500) or in *Śiśupālawadha* of poet Māgha (AD 600 to 800) is a mole mentioned in the *nakha-śikha* section. Yet, in the Indo-Sufi *masnavīs* the mole on the heroine's cheek plays a powerful role. It has been compared to the Pole Star, death, the bearer of poison, and the thing which can burn a person in the fire of *viraha* (love in separation). According to Pandey (1982: 57–76), in the Persian *masnavī* tradition, a mole can inflict pain and injury upon the lover and is always the focus of attention. The interesting part here is that although the *nakha-śikha varṇana* borrows heavily from Indian traditions, it also incorporates descriptions of the heroine's beauty from their Persian contrcounterparts.

After Rūpcand learns of Cāndā's beauty from Bajur, he attacks her father's kingdom to obtain her. Cāndā's father, who was losing, recruits the help of the hero Lorik to get him out of his predicament. At this point, an account of the war follows in some detail. This does not come as a surprise because a fully developed treatment of valour and chivalry (*vīr ras*) is common to the *Shāhnāma, Rāmāyaṇa*, and *Mahābhārata*. These are arguably the works of literature that were most influential in shaping the development of the Indo-Sufi *masnavī* genre.

फरसा कुंत कटारी लीतेहि बांधि चला तरवारि।
रगत पिपासु खांड लोर कर दौरा जीभ पसारि।। (M. Gupta 1967: 106)

(Arming himself) with a hatchet, a dagger, an armour;
and fastening of a sword, bloodthirsty Lorik rushed
forth with his tongue hanging out,
A cutlass (double-edged cleaver) in hand.

To celebrate his victory, Lorik is invited to the royal palace for a banquet. Cāndā and Lorik see each other for the first time and Lorik faints. Doctors who come to see Lorik suspect that he may be lovesick. Cāndā's old nanny goes to visit Lorik in the guise of a *vaidya* at Cāndā's request and arranges a rendezvous at a shrine.

In the Indo-Sufi *masnavī* literature, enlisting the help of an agent is a recurring motif. Often the wise men who are brought to diagnose the illness of the hero or the heroine are unable to remedy the situation. Then a close friend or a confidante, a parrot or some other bird, or a fakir helps point out the way to the beloved. In the following lines, Cāndā is coaching Biraspati (Bṛhaspati) to do certain things for her:

अबहिं जाइ धरि बांह उचावहि।
बिरह बिभूत मुनि पानि पियावहि।
अस जिनि कहहि कि चांद पठाइउं।
पूछत कहिसु सही चलि आइउं।। (M. Gupta 1967: 176)

Go right now and raise him by the arm.
Give the gentleman who is suffering the pangs of separation some water to drink.
Don't say that Cāndā has sent you.
If asked, just say I came to pay a casual visit.

Further in the story, Cāndā again sends a message to Lorik through Biraspati, who goes and says to Lorik

आइ बिरस्पति कहा संदेसु।
लोर चांद लइ चलु परदेसु।। (M. Gupta 1967: 275)

Biraspati came and recited the (following) message:
Lorik, along with Cāndā, move on to another region.

Lorik's wife then sends him a message through a traveller, asking him to return home. In Sanskrit works, the motif of messenger occurs primarily in *dūtakāvya* where the pavana, breeze, serves as a messenger, as in *pavanadūta* of Dhoī, see also the role of the cloud in Kalidas's *Meghadūta*. Also in works such as *Kathāsaritsāgara*, Bāṇbhaṭṭa's *Kādambarī*, as well as in *The Masnavī* of Maulana Rumi and in Attar's *Mantiq al-Tayr*, birds such as the parrot, the mainā and the sīmurgh, play important roles.[15] Sometimes, the lovers request the breeze to act as a messenger.

The role of the breeze as a messenger is a Persian borrowing. The following two couplets in the same meter are from Khazu Kirmani and Hafiz, respectively (Batra 1973: 365):

Ei sabā, khabarī kon, marā az ān, keh tū dānī
Badāñ zamin guzarī kon, dar āñ zamāñ, keh tū dānī.

O, morning breeze, please inform me
Of what is going on that you know of.
Do pass through *that* place,
At such a time, which you think best.

and,

Nasīm-i-subah-i-saādat, bedan niśāñ, keh tū dānī
khabar bakū-i-fulāñ bar badāñ jamāñ, keh tū dānī.

> O benevolent, cool, soft breeze of the morning,
> at that certain address which you know of,
> Do bear a message *to that certain one's* street,
> At an opportune moment, as you see fit.

Intervention, assistance, or a supernatural being who plays an important role are also common. For example, in *Cāndāyan*, the hero is helped by snake charmers to revive Cāndā when she succumbs to snakebites. In *Mṛgāvatī*, the heroine first appears in the form of doe. Then she changes into a nymph. Later the hero tricks her into assuming a human body. From her human form, once again, she changes into a nymph and flies off to her abode. Finally the love, devotion, and commitment of the hero brings her back to the form of a woman.

Similarly, in *Madhumālatī*, the nymphs bring the hero, Prince Manohar, and the heroine, Madhumālatī, together when they are asleep. When the two of them wake up, they fall in love. However, the nymphs are horrified at what has occurred and take the prince back to his kingdom, where he suffers the pangs of separation (*viyoga*) and so begins the allegory of the soul's quest for the divine.

Love in separation (*viraha*) is considered the most poignant of all emotions (*rasa*). In *masnavī* literature the poet does not distinguish between the divine beloved and the beloved of this world. Love in this world is often the means to experience celestial, eternal love. In fact, it is believed that love and beauty in this world are but a means to their everlasting counterparts. Sufi literature lays emphasis on the premise that only those who are sincere in their quest can bear the pain of separation and transcend it to find true love. In the Indo-Sufi *masnavīs*, it is said time and again that enduring the pain of separation is not an ordinary accomplishment. Only those whose passion for the quest is more intense than their concern for their own lives may embark on the path of love.

In Nizami's *Lailā-Majnūn*, the hero unites with his beloved only after his death. Similarly, Farhād dies enduring the pangs of *viraha*. Zulaikha unites with Yusuf only after conquering all desires born of flesh. In *Padmāvat*, to test whether Ratansen's love was true, Pārvatī goes to him in the guise of a nymph and tries to seduce him. Ratansen passes the test. In *Cāndāyan*, Mainā (Lorik's first wife) and, in *Padmāvat*, Nāgamatī (Ratansen's first wife) each burns in the flames of separation in her husband's absence.

After seeing Cāndā, Lorik cannot go back to life in his village. He repudiates his home and life of comfort, and becomes a mendicant. Like a yogi he practices austerities and suffers hardships for a whole year in the forest. At this point, the hero is compared to Śiva, the greatest of the ascetics (Embrace 1988: 262). Later, when he and Cāndā elope, Lorik again fights battles and suffers total poverty. The feature of the hero living like an ascetic is present in most *masnavī* literature. Majnūn and Farhād have to endure desolation, just as the Pāṇḍavas in *Mahābhārata* face exile and wander in the wilderness. In *Cāndāyan*, Lorik compares his suffering to those of Rāma in the *Rāmāyaṇa*. When Cāndā dies from the snakebite, Lorik laments her loss and says that his condition is exactly like that of Rāma, whose wife was taken away from him during his exile in the jungle.

> नाग़ भेस होइ केइ धनि हरी।
> लोरहि राम अवस्था परी।। (M. Gupta 1967: 320)

> In the guise of a cobra, who has stolen my treasure?
> Alas! On Lorik befalls the same calamity (situation) as Rāma.

The suffering of the hero for the sake of the heroine is a feature of the *masnavī* genre as a whole and, because it is an integral component of the *masnavī* genre, it is found in the Persian *masnavīs* such as *Lailā-Majnūn* and *Śīrīn-Farhād*, as well as in the Indo-Sufi *masnavīs* such as *Cāndāyan* and *Padmāvat*. The hero is the symbol of the soul (*ātmā*) and the heroine represents the Supreme Soul (*paramātmā*). The heroine is always illustrative of the divine. Mythological legends aside, raising the status of a woman so high that she represents God is not really typical of the Indian literary tradition.

Granted that 'contradictory views have been expressed concerning the social status of a Hindu woman. On the one hand it is enjoined that she should be shown the utmost respect, on the other, she is said to deserve no freedom' (Embree 1988: 228). Most scholars agree that in traditional Indian literature, women were considered obstacles to man's quest for higher truth.

According to ancient texts such as *Skanda Purāṇa*,[16] whenever an ascetic such as Śiva or Viśvāmitra practised rigorous austerities, Indra, the lord of the gods, would find his throne trembling and feel insecure. He would see his place in the heavens in jeopardy. Consequently, he would send celestial nymphs such as Menakā and Urvaśī to seduce the sage away from the path of *puṇya* and spiritual practices. In the same way, Kāma, god of love, would send beautiful women to tempt Śiva. The nymphs would seduce him so that he would be distracted from his devotion to chastity (Embree 1988: 262).

Discussing the elevated status of women in the Indo-Sufi *masnavī* genre, Bhala Chandra Tiwari writes,

> In the *Mahābhārata*, there is no dearth of examples where women are given adjectives such as illusion, fire-snake, poisonous, thoughtless, fickle, and wicked and are generally neglected. According to Sufi doctrines, to a devotee, God appears in the form of a woman. The Supreme Soul is the beloved, the devotee is the lover. The devotee desires to drink from the cup handed to him by the beloved. He tries to keep the beloved happy and begs for the gift of love. (Tiwari 1936: 3, 11; translation mine)

According to Maya Mishra, in Buddhist canonical literature, women were considered hindrances to the path of sacrifice and reform. Post-Brahmanical cults insisted on renunciation and the sacrifice of family life. Take, for example, in *Saundarānanda*, of Aśvaghoṣa (first century AD), about the conversion of the reluctant Nanda by the Buddha, a story recounted in the *Mahāvagga* and the *Nidānakathā* (Keith 1928: 57). This reduced the importance of a woman's place in society. Compared to this, the bedrock of Sufi teachings is the experience of love. Holding love to be supremely important, the Sufi poets have projected a very high vision of life in their Indo-Sufi *masnavīs*, which transcends the social, moral, religious, and philosophical hang-ups and manifests itself in the most natural and forceful form (M. Mishra 1962: 118–21).

In fact, the treatment of women, and what the heroine in particular stands for in a *masnavī*, contributes to the identity of the Indo-Sufi *masnavī* genre to a very large extent and must be recognized as a significant element.

When Lorik and Cāndā realize that if they wish to be together they will have to leave their respective homes, they take the final step and cross the river. Their journey is a long and uncertain adventure. The following couplet depicts the scene when Lorik and Cāndā are requesting a boatman to take them to the other shore. The boatman in the meantime has other designs on his mind:

> खेवट देखि बिमोहा रूपा।
> अभरन बहुल सो नारि सुरूपा।
> बड़ग गोसाईं पूजइ आसा।
> असि तिरिया जउ आवइ पासा। (M. Gupta 1967: 288)

> When the boatman saw (Cāndā), the one with the lovely form,
> He was enamored. (He thought,) So many ornaments!
> Moreover, the woman is beautiful!
> If such a woman were to be accessible, [literally, 'were to come near'],
> O Lord, This would be the culmination of all hopes and desires.

During their adventures, sometimes Lorik and Cāndā receive hospitality and, at other times, they are treated as strangers and enemies. Twice Cāndā succumbs to snakebites, leaving Lorik distraught and ready to give up his life with her. At one point Lorik decides to die on Cāndā's funeral pyre holding her in an embrace.

चांद कांध लै सरि पहुंचाई।
आनी आगि चाहि बर जाई।। (M. Gupta 1967: 325)

Resting Cāndā on his shoulders, (Lorik) took her to the pyre,
Igniting the fire, he wanted to burn (in that fire).

Total and complete commitment to the beloved was mandatory for the heroes of *masnavī* literature. All lovers have to go through the test of unconditional love. In Nizamī's works, Majnūn and Farhād lose their lives in their quest. Lorik and Ratansen also risk their lives seeking union with their loved ones.

Back in the village, Mainā, Lorik's wife, suffers during her husband's absence and so does Lorik's mother. This part which describes the suffering of Mainā comes through in the second *bārahmāsā* in the text, separate from the portion describing Cāndā's sufferings. The following pertains to Mainā's sufferings in Lorik's absence from home:

बिरह संताई मैना एहिं परि दिन अउ राति।
संइहि लीन्हे दुख लोरिकहिं केरा बिरहा संघाति।। (M. Gupta 1967: 339)

Tormented by the pain of love in separation,
Mainā suffered day and night this way.
She involuntarily endured the grief (inflicted) by Lorik,
viraha (anguish of separation) struck her down with a heavy blow.

Following Lorik's elopement with Cāndā, Mainā's life is turned around, but she remains faithful to her husband, *satī*, and true to her *dharma*. Many months later, she meets a traveller going in the same direction where, from what she had heard from other travellers, she thought Lorik might be. She and Lorik's mother, Kholin, send their entreaties to Lorik and Cāndā to come home. When the traveller reaches Lorik with the message, after four months on the road, Lorik and Cāndā head back.

Parallel to the description of love in separation, there is the test of sincerity. Sometimes the hero, sometimes the heroine must go through this test. More often it is the fate of the first wife. This demonstrates an affinity with the story of Sītā (the wife of Rāma) and her trial by fire (*agniparīkṣā*). In *Cāndāyan*, when Lorik elopes with Cāndā, his wife Mainā manages the household in his absence and looks after her mother-in-law. They are reduced to poverty and she has to sell dairy products door-to-door. When Lorik returns to his village, he wants to make sure that his wife has remained true to him in his absence. In the guise of being Cāndā's spouse, he tries to flirt with her. Mainā gives him a piece of her mind.

जइं का दीखि हउं बेसा दारी।
तहं तू मों सउं करसि धमारी।। (M. Gupta 1967: 389)

Do I appear to you a whore or a woman to be used?
(Of course not). Then how (dare) you cavort with me?

When Mainā and Cāndā come face-to-face, there is a struggle between them similar to the one described earlier in the story.

बर कइ चांदइ झूझ उपावा।
भया झूझ जस दाउद गावा।। (M. Gupta 1967: 392)

Cāndā got upset and started a fight. A struggle,
Just like the one Daud described before, ensued.

Eventually reconciliation takes place and both live in harmony. According to Umapati Chandel (1976: 278–80), in the Indo-Sufi *masnavīs*, very often the hero stays with the heroine's family for a protracted period of time. Then he receives a message from the first wife and is eager to go home immediately. The episode when the hero, after a long absence from his homeland receives a message which prompts an immediate response, is common to many literary traditions. In Kalidasa's *Śākuntalam*, after a long absence from home, King Duṣyanta hastily returns to his capital after receiving a message. In *Padmāvat*, Raja Ratansen also hurries home after receiving a letter from his capital.

According to a story associated with the Persian poet Rudaki's composition, *Cahār maqāla*, the king was on an expedition which kept him busy for a long time. His absence caused concern in the capital. The ministers called upon the skills of Rudaki (d. 954) to bring the king back. According to the legend, Rudaki composed a poem which would remind the king of the familiar scenes from around his capital. When the poem was read to the king, he was so overcome with homesickness, he mounted his horse and rode home. The poem in question begins as follows:

Bū-i jū-i mūliyān, āyad hamīn,
Bū-i-yār-i-mehrabān, āyad hamīn.

Its translation is as follows:

The jū-i-Muliyāñ we call to mind,
We long for those dear friends long left behind.
The sands of Oxus, toilsome though they be,
Beneath my feet were soft as silk to me.
Glad at the friends's return, the Oxus deep
Up to our girths in laughing waves shall leap.
Long live Bukhārā! Be though of good cheer!
Joyous towards thee hasteth our Amīr!
The Moon's the Prince, Bukhārā is the sky;
O sky, the Moon shall light thee by and by!
Bukhārā is the mead, the Cypress he;
Receive at last, O Mead, the Cypress-tree! (Browne 1928: 15).

When Lorik receives Mainā's message in *Cāndāyan*, he sets out homeward. In many later *masnavīs*, the hero leaves the father-in-law's home and embarks on a return journey along with the heroine. The send-off usually is accompanied by great pomp and ceremony. In some Indo-Sufi *masnavīs* the hero's boat meets storms or other difficulties. However, in the end, he arrives home safely.

When the first wife and the heroine have to live together, there is mutual jealousy. In some *masnavīs, Puhupāvatī*, for example, three wives have to live together in harmony. At times, to find his beloved, the hero, who may be unmarried, has to marry a princess to enlist her help. In this situation, also the question of mutual jealousy arises (Chandel 1976: 279).

It is important to keep in mind that the Indo-Sufi *masnavīs* are much more than ordinary love stories. On one level, there is romance and adventure for entertainment, interesting at face value. At another level, deep messages are being imparted by means of symbolism. Lorik is the symbol of the soul (*ātman*), eternally in quest of unity with the Supreme Soul (*paramātman*). The heroine represents God. When the hero leaves home in search of the beloved, he creates a distance between his worldly life (*ihalaukika jīvan*) and his spiritual existence (*ādhyātmika jīvan*). However, when he comes back to his previous life, which represents the worldly aspect of his existence, initially he has to struggle but eventually he does find a balance between the two.

The last thematic feature of Indo-Sufi *masnavī* literature concerns the concluding portion of the composition and its message. In the closing portion of *Padmāvat*, Malik Muhammad Jayasi provides the reader a key to the symbols he has used. *Cāndāyan*, as we know, is not as yet available in its complete form, and we do not know if such a clarification accompanied the original text. In the 538th *kaḍvak* of *Madhumālatī*, the poet extolls the virtue of love. Only love is capable of conquering death; it is the exclusive vehicle capable of providing access to immortality. Similarly, in *Mṛgāvatī*, in the last *kaḍvak*, #427, the poet tells the reader that the only important thing in life with lasting beneficial results is total devotion to God.

अहिनिसि जपहु छाडि सब काजा।
अंत रहहि ओकर पै राजा।। (*Mṛgāvatī* 1968: 427)

Leaving aside all other occupations,
Chant (His name) day and night.
In the end, only His reign
will remain unshakeable.

According to Pandey, the description of the environment and the sequence in which the story progresses, are standard elements in the Indo-Sufi *masnavī* genre that where within the traditional framework (Pandey 1982: 321). In conclusion, the thematic features of *masnavī* literature in general remain fairly constant and demonstrate many features retained from the Persian *masnavī* tradition, along with elements borrowed, improvised, and elaborated from the existing Indic literary tradition.

Metrical Structure

In order to examine if, and how far, early Indian Sufi poetry written in dialects of Hindi (in general) and *Cāndāyan* (in particular) conform to the Indic or Persian poetic frameworks, we need first to examine the rules for the *mahākāvya*. We shall then examine corresponding patterns in the Persian *masnavī*.

As mentioned earlier, the meter in a *mahākāvya* changes after each *sarga*, giving the poet an opportunity to show off his creative ease in more than one meter. The text of the poem is divided into shorter sections and the major emotions or *rasas* are explored.

On a cursory glance, it appears that, except for maintaining a single stanza form throughout the entire narrative, most early Sufi narrative poems generally conform to the basic rules of a *mahākāvya*, and Dwivedi and Rajnath Sharma identify *Padmāvat* as a Hindi *mahākāvya*. But closer examination makes it quite evident that in terms of prosody, in the composition of the Indo-Sufi *masnavīs*, all the prescribed rules are *not* completely adhered to. This is more true in the case of *Cāndāyan*, the earliest extant narrative of this genre. Although technically the text of *Cāndāyan* is divided into smaller sections called *kaḍvak* (described in detail below), the *kaḍvak* in *Cāndāyan* functions more like a paragraph than a chapter. It is therefore quite different from a *sarga*, 'canto', in both form and function.

Is *Cāndāyan*, therefore, a *masnavī* in the Persian sense of the term? The following five meters, *hajaz, ramal, sarī'a, khafīf* and *mutaqārib* are designated for the composition of a Persian *masnavī*. Nizami's *Khusrau-Śīrīn* and *Lailā-Majnūn* are composed in *hajaz*; Attar's *Mantik ut-Tair* and Rumi's *Masnavī* in *ramal; sarī'a* is the meter of *Makhzan-i-asrār* of Maulana Nizami; Hakim Sanai's *Hadīqat ul-Haqīqat* is composed in the *khafīf* meter; and Firdausi's *Śāhnama* is in *mutaqārib*.[17] Any given Persian *masnavī* is composed in a single meter. Although it is true that in emulating the Persian models, *Cāndāyan* does not change the meter at the end of each section, it does not borrow from the Persian prosody.

This said, it must nevertheless be made clear that though not used for the *masnavī*, a stanza form comparable to that of *Cāndāyan* did exist in the Persian ode or *qasīda*. Heshmat Moayyad writes, 'Manuchehri of Damghan (d. 1040) is said to have introduced a new stanzaic form, the *mosammat* (aaaaab cccccb, etc.) in Persian poetry, specificially in the *qasīda* or the ode genre during the Ghaznavid period' (Moayyad 1987: 127–30). All poetic lines were equal. Perhaps Mulla Daud, in his choice of five *chaupāī* followed by a *dohā*, was influenced by the *qasīdā* form.

Since *Cāndāyan* does not conform to all the rules prescribed for either the *mahākāvya* or the *masnavī*, one might wonder if its author perhaps intentionally synthesized the melody and rhythm of Indic and Persian epic traditions. In other words, to enhance the texture and fabric of his tapestry, he carefully selected and interwove the delicate threads of the local folklore, the Persian pattern, and popular meters. He thereby imbued *Cāndāyan* with balance and lasting beauty.

Discussing the complex subject of prosody in the preface of his edition of *Cāndāyan*, Mataprasad Gupta states, 'As far as the prosody is concerned, it is entirely Indian. In *Cāndāyan*, neither the meter of the Persian *masnavī* is used nor is the model of completing the entire epic in one single meter maintained' (M. Gupta 1967: 15). The term *masnavī* is used for Sufi narrative poems in Awadhi, referring mostly to the genre of the 'narrative poem' rather than a work that follows the Persian meter.

At this point, we must take a look at the frameworks developed in India to examine to what extent existing taxonomies are useful in accounting for or describing the actual metric practice of early Hindu-Sufi poets.

The body of literature pertaining to the subject of prosody of Old, Middle, and New Indo-Aryan literature is surprisingly large. The majority of the OIA, MIA, and NIA poetic compositions can be divided into two primary categories, *vārṇika chanda* and *mātrika chanda*, or syllabic and moric verse. The first is measured by the quantity of syllables, the second by the number of syllables in a line. Moric verse follows rules where value is assigned by quantity based on vowel length, single or combined consonants, etc. In classical prosody, the line comprises a fixed number of trisyllabic feet, *gaṇas*, with different combinations of long and short syllables.[18]

Syllabic meter prevailed in Vedic literature and classical Sanskrit *Kāvya*. Consequently, even modern books on the subject of prosody still describe at length the classical *vārṇik* meters, despite the fact that for the last 800 years, the majority of the vernacular poetic literature has been composed in *mātrik chandas*. Recently, however, there has been emphasis on the *vārṇik* and *mātrik chandas*. This break with tradition is reflected in the number of pages dedicated to the treatment of the respective *chandas* as well as the location within the discussion of the *chanda*. For example, in *Vāgya Vimarś* of Visvanath Prasad Mishra (1965), *Alaṁkār Pārijāta* of Narottam Das Swami (1969), *Prabandha Prasūna* of Baburao Joshi (1966), and *Rasa, Chanda, Alaṁkāra* of Kṛṣṇadeva Śarmā (1965), the subject of *chanda* is addressed in the old-fashioned way: the *vārṇik chanda* is described first and takes up several pages before the subject of the *mātrik chanda* is brought to the reader's attention. Compared to the above, *Kāvyālocan* of Omprakash Shastri (1967) and *Kāvyaṁg Darpaṇ* of Vijay Avasthi (1972) give the well-deserved and long overdue recognition to the *mātrik chanda*. This marks a break from the traditional method of addressing the subject of prosody in Hindi and expresses an effort to catch up with the existing disjunction.

However, all the above-mentioned texts still rely on the earlier works on meter such as *Prakṛta paiṅgalaṁ, Chandonuśāsan, Vṛttaratnākara, Chandoratnākara* (Sharma 1967: 292–3). These texts, written for languages other than Hindi, are still cited and, despite the fact that the *vārṇik chanda* does not have much Hindi poetic literature to its credit, all the above texts do mention the *vārṇik chanda* and have not broken completely with tradition. Only recently a few European scholars have recognized the *mātrik chanda* as the popular vehicle of Hindi poetic literature.[19]

In the *mātrik chanda*, the basic principle is governed by the time it takes to articulate a short (I), or a long (S), syllable. There is general agreement among scholars that even within the rules that define and subdivide the various *mātrik chandas*, the poet is allowed more creative freedom in the moric system. A large number of the poetic compositions in Prākṛt, Apabhraṁśa, Awadhī, Braj, Hindi, and vernacular languages are composed in *mātrik chanda*. One very important feature to keep in mind in this system is the free movement of the *mātrās* within a given moric poetic meter. For example, in a couplet each line should have 16 *mātrās*; only the quantity of the rhyme is fixed.

The Meter in *Cāndāyan*

Cāndāyan is written as a succession of uniform stanzas. Stanzas in narrative poetry in Awadhī are usually referred to as *kaḍvaks*, a term also used for Apabhraṁśa narrative stanzas. The term is of uncertain origin—perhaps related to *kaṛā/kaṛī* in the sense of 'link' (*kaḍa*). We will come to the details regarding the form of the *kaḍvak* shortly.

Because *Cāndāyan* is the earliest extant composition of the Indo-Sufi *masnavī* genre, in the aspects of prosody and language it has served as a model for later *masnavīs*. Surviving oral versions of the story simply consist of long strings of couplets. In the written text, the composition is divided into stanzas called *kaḍvaks*. Thus, the monotony of a single meter is broken by finishing the stanza with a couplet in a different meter at the end of each *kaḍvak*.

Additionally in *Cāndāyan*, each stanza or *kaḍvak* has an introductory, non-metrical sentence in Persian indicating the contents of the following stanza. This unique feature, called *surkhiyān* (rubric), is found in the earliest (1525) available manuscript of *Cāndāyan* and may therefore be considered an integral part of the text.

The stanzas used in *Cāndāyan* comprise two very popular meters, *caupāī* and *dohā*. After five lines of *caupāī*, a *dohā* follows, which makes up a *kaḍvak*. The *caupāī* is a rhyming couplet of two sixteen *mātrā* lines. The *dohā* is a rhyming couplet, each of the two lines containing 24 *mātrās*. Each line is further divided into two feet. The first and the third feet of a *dohā* have 13 *mātrās* each and the second and the fourth contain 11 *mātrās* each. There is disagreement among prominent scholars of

Hindi prosody such as Mahesh and Kellogg about the exact number of *mātrās* in each of the four feet of the *caupāī* (Asani 1991: 106).

Given that pre-existent metrical frameworks are not adequate for characterizing the metrical structure of *Cāndāyan*, the question arises as to how best to characterize the metrical structure of the work. Parmeshvarilal Gupta suggests that Daud, and, to some extent, Jayasi, modelled their compositions after the metric patterns of the Apabhraṁśa narratives and adapted the *kaḍvak* unit from there. P. Gupta (1964: 31–5) suggests that Daud could have followed the descriptions of the *kaḍvak* units given in works such as Swayambhū's *Svayambhū Chandas* and Hemacandra's *Chandonuśāsan,* and used for narrative poems such as *Ṇāyakumāracariu.*

According to Swayambhū, each *kaḍvak* must contain eight *yamaka* lines followed by a couplet of *dhruva/dhruvaka* or *chaḍanika*, also called *dhattā*. Sinha writes, 'Our poets and prosodists have tried to name or rename different meters. That means that different names have been given to the same meters by different authors or that the same name is given to a different meter. This habit has continued up to this day' (Mahesh 1964: 17).

A *yamaka* consists of two feet, each containing 16 *mātrās*, and is equivalent to the later *caupāī* of the Indo-Sufi *masnavīs*. The three major variations of this meter are the following:

> *Paddhika*: Each foot contains 16 *mātrās*. 1S1 is the end rhyme.
>
> *Vadanaka*: Each foot contains 16 *mātrās*. S11 and sometimes SS is the end rhyme.
>
> *Paranaka*: Consists of 15 *mātrās*. 111 or 1S is the usual end rhyme (M. Gupta 1964: 36).

In practice, these rules are not rigidly adhered to. Thus one finds ample examples of Apabhraṁśa poetry where a *kaḍvak* may contain any number of *yamakas* between 20 to 25.

Despite the prescribed number of *yamakas* for a *kaḍvak* being eight, in *Cāndāyan*, each *kaḍvak*, to use Swayambhū's terminology, consists of five *yamakas* followed by a *dhattā*. This pattern is consistent throughout the composition. A similar stanza form was used in later Awadhi narrative poems, though the number of *caupāī* lines varies. For example, Malik Muhammad Jayasi adopted seven *caupāī* lines followed by a *dohā* to make up a *kaḍvak* for his *Padmāvat*.

Technically, a *dhatta* could consist of two to six feet. But in *Cāndāyan* routinely a *dhattā* has four feet. There are three main varieties of *dhattās*:

(a) all four feet have an equal number of *mātrās*, or (b) the first two feet have the same number of *mātrās*. (The third and the fourth feet have the same number of *mātrās* but the number of *mātrās* in the second and the third feet are not the same.), (c) The number of *mātrās* in the first and the third feet and second and fourth feet are the same. The *dohā* conforms to the last of these. Theoretically there are scores of possible variations (number of *mātrās* varying anywhere between seven to seventeen) of *dhattās* depending on the *mātrā* arrangements.

Clearly, if the laws of the metrical patterns of the *yamakas* and the *dhattās* as prescribed by Swayambhū are applied to *Cāndāyan*, it becomes evident that early Indo-Sufi poets used a strophic form not accounted for in the treatises on prosody.

Let us take a few examples of this poetry and see whether it conforms to the analytic frameworks discussed above. If these frameworks are not suitable for the text(s) in question, let us consider alternative approaches.

We begin with a representative example of a *kaḍvak* from Puṣpadanta's (d. 972) *Ṇāyakumāracariu*. This is in order to establish the fact that the *kaḍvak* of *Cāndāyan* relates to earlier usage of the *kaḍvak* pattern in Apabhraṁśa narrative poetry:

तओ मुणिंदजंपियं मणे वरं थिरं थियं।
सुतारहारपंडुरं गया सई समंदिरं।
णिबद्धणीलतोरणं विचित्तमत्तवारणं।
सुहेमभित्तिपिंगलं अणेयगेयमंगलं।
तहिं सिणिद्धवण्णिया णरिंदविंदवण्णिय।
कइंदविंदवण्णिया सुहासणे णिसण्णिया।
वणे पहू पहिटठओ सरोवरं पहिटठओ।
पलोइयं सरोरूहं वियंभियं पियामुहं।
पहंतरं णिहालिरो ण जंपएणरेसरो।
विलासिणीसिंह सित्तओ णिमीलियंच्छिवित्तओ।
थिओ वियारवज्जिओ ण नीससंतु लज्जिओ।
णीलुप्पलपहओ हरिसहो ण गओ णरवइणियमणि भावइ।
जियकलहंसिणिया पियभासिणिया पहविदेवि किं णावइ ।।5।।

In the above *kaḍvak* there are eleven couplets of 12 *mātrās*, followed by a couplet of 18̄12 *mātrās*. Interestingly, *Ṇāyakumāracariyu* has many *kaḍvaks* that are different from each other. For example, the *kaḍvak* entitled 'March to Girinagara' has 20 couplets of ten *mātrās* followed by a couplet of 11$\bar{1}$1 *mātrās* but the *kaḍvak* entitled 'Nāgakumār's chivalrous response' has 6 couplets of 14 *mātrās* followed by 11$\bar{1}$3. Additionally, there are 'stanzas' not followed by a *dhattā* but separated by a rubric (Jain 1944).

The following is an example of a *kaḍvak* from *Cāndāyan* (M. Gupta 1967: 346) with its metrical scansion and translation. The only purpose of this example is to demonstrate that neither in the Apabhraṁśa *kāvya* above nor in the early Sufi-Hindi poems, does the number of *yamakas* conform to the rules. The number of *caupāīs*, 5 in this case and 12 in the above *kaḍvak*, clearly differs from Swayambhū's rule of 8 lines of *yamakas* in a *kaḍvak*:

छाडेउं भाइ बाप महतारी। तजेउं बियाही मैना नारी।।1
slls, lslll, ss, llls, sss, ss (16$\bar{1}$6)
I abandoned (my) brother, father, and mother.
I repudiated Maina, (my) wedded woman.

लोग कुटंब घर बार बिसारेउं। देख छाडि परदेस सिधारेउं।।2
slll, llsll, sll (16). slsl, llsll, sll (16).
I forgot (my) clansmen, house and portal.
Leaving my country I set-off for other lands.

गाउं ठाउं पोखर अंबराई। परिहरि निसरेउं कवन उपाई।।3
slsl, sllll, ss (16). lllll, lllll, ss (16).
(My) village, abode, lake, and mango groves,
How I gave them up, deeming them to be insubstantial.

अरथ दरब का लोभ न कीहेउं। चांद सनेह देसन्तर लीन्हेउं।।4
llllll, ssll, sll (16). slls, llsll, sll (16).
I did not lust after money or material things.
I embraced banishment for Cāndā's love.

बिच होइ बाट परी करतारा। न धनि भयेउ न मीत पियारा।।5
llls, llsll, ss (16). lllll, llsll, ss (16).
O God, (what calamity) befell us in the middle of the road.
Neither remain the riches, or the beloved friend.

भई बात अब जानेउं चांदा, तोरै मरन निदान।।6
lssl, llsll, ss, sslllsl (16+11)
O Cāndā, (only) after your demise I have realized,

जो जिउ जाइ कया कस देखहि, मै का करब अबाग।।7
slls, llsll, sll ssllllsl (16+11)

If life departs, how can the form (remain to) be seen.
Stupid me, (disarmed/helpless), what can I do?

The last couplet, as is evident, does not conform to the definition of a *dohā*.[20]

Now follow a couple of examples of *dhattās* (taken from the *kaḍvaks* #27 and 108 respectively in M. Gupta (1967) in *Cāndāyan* to demonstrate the variations found in the number of their *mātrās*:

खांड चिरौंजी दाख खुरहुरी, बैठे लोग बिसाह। (16+11)
हीर पटोर सौ भल कापड, जित चाहे सब आह।। (15+11)

and

देहु असीस रोचन, मार बांठ घर आउं।
सोने बेडि गढाइ, मोतिहिं मांग भराउं।। (11, 11)

Thus, *dhattā* is not always a *dohā* but a short couplet. This difference between the practice and the principles of prosody has kept the scholars of *Cāndāyan* puzzled. P. Gupta believes that perhaps a better manuscript of *Cāndāyan* may come to light in the future, and he would like to reserve his comments on the topic of this disparity.

For his part Pathak states:

> In agreement with Mataprasad Gupta's statement that the Sufi poets have taken great liberties with the traditional forms of *caupāī* and *dohās*, I have to say the following: Sometimes there is less and sometimes more than the prescribed number of *mātrās* in the poetic compositions of the Sufi poets such as Daud, Jayasi, and Qutuban. This disparity could either be due to editorial mistakes, or because we do not know the actual contemporary pronunciation of certain words used in these compositions. Moreover, the fact that most of the manuscripts were originally written down in the Persian writing system and were later converted to the Nagari system without adequate editorial work adds to the above mentioned difficulty. (Pathak 1978: 252–3)

The form of a *kaḍvak* remained flexible in the years following the composition of *Cāndāyan*. Qutuban's *Mṛgāvatī* (1560), Manjhan's *Madhumālatī* (1602), and Alif Khan Jan's *Kanakāvatī* (1678) have *kaḍvaks* of five *chaupāīs* followed by a *dohā*. Jayasi composed his *Padmāvat* (1597) in a stanza of seven *chaupāī* followed by a *dohā*. Many other works such as Usman's *Citrāvali* (1670) follow this pattern.

With the passage of time, however, this disparity was corrected in the emerging genre of long narrative poems and poetry a few decades

Fig. 1: Entrance and congregation area at the entrance of a Sufi khanqāh. (Recently renovated and refurbished by Govt. of India, Dept. of Tourism, Patna). (Photograph by the author.)

Fig. 2: The Maner manuscript . . . khanqāh (monastery) of Maner (Bihar). (Photograph by the author.)

Fig. 3: Peer's dargah (Maner *khanqāh*). (Photograph by the author.)

Fig. 4: The colourful city of Dalmau flourished with forts on the hills, the Ganges flowing below. (Photograph by the author.)

after *Cāndāyan* followed closer to Swayambhū's rules. For example, the following is a *kaḍvak* from the *Rāmacaritamānas* of Tulsidas. Most scholars agree that the composition of the *Mānas* began approximately in 1574–75. When compared with the earlier *masnavīs*, it is evident that Tulsidas certainly selected the number of *yamakas* as prescribed (i.e. eight):

जो मुनीश जेहि आयसु दीन्हा। सो तेहि काज प्रथम जनु कीन्हा।।
s lsl 11sll ss, s ll sl lll ll ss (16͞16)

विप्र साधु सुर पूजत राजा। करत राम हित मंगलकाजा।।
ls sl ll sll ss, lll sl ll lsl ss (16͞16)

सुनत राम अभिषेक सुहावा। बाज गहागह अवध बधावा।।
राम सीय तनु सगुन जनाये। फरकहिं मंगल अंग सुहाये।।
पुलकि सप्रेम परस्पर कहहीं। भरत आगमन सूचक अहहीं।।
भये बहुत दिन अवसेरी। सगुन प्रतीत भेंट प्रिय केरी।।
भरत सरिस प्रिय को जग माहीं। इहइ सगुन फलु दूसर नाहीं।।
रामहिं बंधु सोच दिन राति। अंडन्हि कमठ हृदय जेहि भांती।।
एहि अवसर मंगलु परम, सुनि रहसेउ रनिवांसु।
ll llll lsl lll (13), 11 llll llsl (11)

शोभत लखि विधु बढत जनु, वारिधि बीचि बिलासु।। (118 अयोध्याकान्ड)
sll ll ll lll ll (13), sll sl lsl (11)

In short, to try to justify or fit the early Indo-Sufi narrative poems to the exact guidelines or frameworks provided by the prosodic rules is a difficult task because none of these frameworks is entirely suitable for the Indo-Sufi *masnavī*, least of all for *Cāndāyan*. This difference between theory and practice has posed problems for scholars for a number of years. In scanning, even if the *anusvāras* are actually *anunāsikas*, counted as units of varying value, the metrical pattern does not always conform to the prescribed forms. In scanning the *kaḍvak* from *Cāndāyan*, according to Entwistle, -e- is *optionally* short before -u- (-eu in all cases ll; bhayeu seems to be lll and hoi ll rather than Sl because long vowels can be counted short when followed by another vowel. In line 4b perhaps *deśaṁtara* should be lsll. This simply means that depending on their placement certain units can be of varying value.

On this problem Asani says, 'When a student is faced with the task of analysing the functional aspects of prosody in a work of Indic poetry, the traditional methodology available is not adequate' (Asani 1991: 101). Later narrative poems in Awadhī have stanzas comprising 5 to 10 *caupāīs* plus a *dohā*. For example, Nisar's *Yusuf-Zulaikhā* (1874) has 9 *chaupāīs* and a *dohā*; Alaf Khan Jan's *Madhukar-Mālatī* (1691) has 22 *chaupāīs* followed by a *dohā*.

Kenneth Bryant, who has done extensive work on prosody in Braj lyrical poems, writes, 'The problem is that we simply have no ready vocabulary, no descriptive shortcuts, for analysis of this sort; with the tools currently available, a prosodic analysis of any sophistication must be a slow, blow-by-blow affair. . . . In short, what is needed is nothing less than a major reappraisal of medieval North Indian metrics' (Bryant 1978: 132).

Additionally, Bryant has worked on new patterns of internal rhymes and stresses, not very obvious at first glance. These rhymes appear to be in agreement with the musical cycles suitable for, or specifically prescribed for, a given lyrical composition. He has also discussed in detail the regular emerging patterns of stress and strain of the melodic system when applied to medieval Hindi lyrical poetry (Bryant 1992: 209–24).

In conclusion, the observation can be made that the *kaḍvak* of *Cāndāyan* relates to earlier usage in Apabhraṁśa compositions. In other words, the practice of composing in a poetic unit which consists of several *yamaka* lines and ends in a *dhattā* was already in use in the Apabhraṁśa *kāvyas*.[21] The poets of the Indo-Sufi *masnavīs* simply adopted this practice. In time the number of *yamakas* and the *dhattā* which together formed a *kaḍvak* for any given work became standardized. For example, in *Padmāvat* and *Mṛgāvatī*, the number of *yamakas* is not the same. In *Padmāvat* the *dhattā* comes after seven lines of *yamaka* whereas in *Mṛgāvatī*, *dhattā* follows after only five *yamaka* lines. However, once the *kaḍvak* pattern is selected, more or less, the *masnavī* keeps it up from one end to the other.[22] Later narrative compositions in Awadhī demonstrate a remarkable uniformity in their *kaḍvak* design. For example, *Rāmacaritamānas* of Tulasi strictly adheres to the Swayambhu rules, i.e. eight lines of *yamaka* followed by a *dohā*.

NOTES

1. Shyam Manohar Pandey is the leading scholar of the oral tradition and regional variations in the folk versions of the tale of Cāndā and Lorik. The numerous texts of the folk traditions and the location where they were collected are published in S.M. Pandey's *The Hindi Oral Epic Lorikī*, 1979.

2. F.E. Keay, *Hindi Literature*. The statement that 'all else is strictly veracity' perhaps is too strong.
3. See Umapati Chandel's discussion on *Sufi premākhyānak kāvyoṁ kī puarāṇik kathānak rūḍiyāṁ* (1976: 272–310).
4. In this study I use *sarga* and 'canto' interchangeably.
5. Rumi's Spiritual Couplets, in many ways the prime example of the genre, are different in this particular regard.
6. It should be mentioned here that *nūr* or light is an epithet of God (Koran 24: 35).
7. The name of the poets and the dates of their *masnavīs* have been provided in Table 1.1.
8. For details see Nizami Ganjavi 1993.
9. By 'digressions' I mean those stories which are 'asides' within an ongoing discourse, in order to settle a given issue. By 'spin-offs' I mean the retelling of those stories which are originally from well-known texts and are celebrated by reader and/or audience, and which are adopted, adapted, or changed to a degree to suit the immediate purpose of the storyteller.
10. Muhammad Sadiq discusses this practice in great detail in the first volume of his *History of Classical Urdu Literature* (1964).
11. See Narang 1990.

    खुसरौ ऐसी पीत कर जैसे हिंदू जोय
    पूत पराए कारने जल जल कोयला होय

    See also B. Tiwari (1985).
12. For details on Nur al-Din Abd al-Rahman Jami, see Levy 1969: 158–60.
13. Perhaps it is the result of following the model of *Cāndāyan* that the heroines of many of the subsequent Indo-Sufi *masnavīs* continued to belong to the *padmini* class of women, as was the case with most heroines in the Sanskrit *Kāvya* literature.
14. Batra (1973: 666) discusses in detail the many stories in Indo-Sufi *masnavī* literature borrowed from the Persian tradition and traces their original sources. Most often these stories refer to a chapter in the Koran, a legend, or an event from Persian history. The fainting of the hero or beggar in the *masnavī* literature goes all the way back of Moses. The Indian version is as follows: When Moses was passing through the wilderness of Tīh, on his way from Madyan to Egypt, he saw a light on Mount Sinai (Tūr). When he went closer, he saw that a green tree was aflame. He heard a voice which said to him, 'I am your God, O Moses'. Moses asked that he might see God. But he got the answer, 'You cannot see me'. Nonetheless, Moses was insistent. As soon as God showed Moses his magnificent splendour, Moses, unable to see, swooned and fell over. Mount Sinai began to tremble, and, in fact, it actually burnt to cinders. For actual text see Koran, 7/ 143.
15. For *Kathāsaritsāgara*, see Speyer 1908. For more information on the *Kādambarī*, see Keith 1928: 319–26; *The Masnavī*: Nicholson 1977(a). 17–21. For a

commentary on the spiritual birds that are divine Intelligences see Attar 1984: 84–8.

16. See Winternitz 1981: 545.
17. See Batra 1973: 471–7 for details.
18. For more with regard to cataloguing the various combinations of trisyllabic units see *Sanskrit Prosody and Numerical Symbols* by C.P. Brown (1981).
19. 'Prosody in the Modern Indian Vernaculars', in *Princeton Encylopoedia of Poetry and Poetics* (Entwistle 1993) and *A Manual of Urdu Metre*, an unpublished study by C. Shackle (1988).
20. For different readings of the Bombay and England manuscript, see P. Gupta's edition of *Cāndāyan* (1964: 274). In M. Gupta's *Cāndāyan* (1967) it is *kaḍvak* #315.
21. See Jain 1944: xxxix.
22. An exception to this observation can be found in *Cāndāyan*. *Kaḍvak* consisting of different numbers of *yamakas* do occur, but not on a regular basis.

4

The Sufi Content of the Indo-Islamic *Masnavī*

To exemplify the Indo-Sufi *masnavī* in its original Sufi context, it is necessary to become familiar with the tenets and practices of Sufism.[1] I shall limit my discussion to those aspects of Sufism that bear on the interpretation of the Indo-Sufi *masnavī*. In this chapter, my argument will deal primarily with the concept of the 'journey' in Sufi practice and belief, because the narrative is but an allegorical tale of a soul's odyssey for spiritual reunion with the Supreme Soul. The motif of journey is common to both the Persian as well as the Indo-Sufi *masnavī*.

Originally the term *sūfī*[2] was applied to those who had been the companions of the Prophet and assembled with him to pray in the same row (*saf*). According to Chandra Bali Pandey:

> There used to be a little platform (*suffā*) adjacent to the Madina mosque. Holy men who put up there were called the 'Sufis'. Yet another view on the origin of the term 'Sufi' is that on the day of judgement, those who have loved God and have made sacrifices along the path which leads to God will be assembled in a separate and distinguished row (*saf*). Those who belong in this row are the Sufi. (C.B. Pandey 1966: 7)

It was also believed that one who practised piety and was constantly in the pursuit of spiritual purification was a Sufi (*sof*). According to some scholars, the word *sufi* is derived from the Arabic *sūf* meaning 'wool', with a Persian derivational suffix 'i'.

Until recently the derivation of the word *sūfi* was in dispute. Most Sufis, flying in the face of etymology, have derived it from an Arabic root which conveys the notion of 'purity'; this would make *sūfi* 'one who is pure in heart' or 'one of the elect'. Some European scholars have identified *sūfi* with 'theosophist' (Nicholson 1975: 5).

Annemarie Schimmel agrees that the word *sūfi* is derived from the Arabic root which means 'wool'.

> It is conceivable that the inner life of Islam might have been suffocated in the ever-narrowing net of dogmatic definitions and scholastic methods, or in the external ritual and legal prescriptions which seemed to increase almost year to year. However, a new current, mysticism, appeared in the world of Islam and gave it, in many areas, a special form. This mystical current is called Sufism, a word derived from *suf*, 'wool'. From this term one can understand the originally ascetic character of the movement, for just as early Christian ascetics in the Near East used to wear woollen cloaks, thus early Muslims ascetics, too, donned a dark, usually dark blue, woollen garb. (Schimmel 1992: 101)

In the early years of Islam, the common man felt its appeal and united under its banner to claim a life of principles, discipline, and decency. In the years after the Prophet passed away (632), some of the men who had come from relatively modest backgrounds declared themselves rulers of large territories. Disregarding the model of the Prophet, who had lived a life of austerity and asceticism, these Arab citizens became rulers, *khalīfās*, of Syria, Iraq, and Iran and began to lead a life of luxury and decadence. However, some of the members of the Islamic community continued to practice poverty, *faqr*. Their open criticism against material accumulation of those who were in powerful positions brought unfortunate consequences. Ali, the Prophet's cousin, was assassinated and most of his family was finally massacred at Karbalā. These atrocities on the part of the ruling hierarchies made many of followers of the tenets of Islam more firm in their determination to preserve their religion in its original pure form and spirit.

Concerning the historical background against which Sufism, the mystical movement in Islam, came about, Schimmel says:

> Soon after the era of the four righteous califs ended in 661, the ruling family of Umayyads moved their capital from Arabia to Syria. In 750 the Abbasids who came to power moved their capital to Baghdad. The Abbasid period is considered the heyday of Muslim civilization, literature and art. At the same time, the more pious Muslims turned to stricter asceticism-in opposition to the growing luxury of everyday life. (Schimmel 1993: 3–4)

Hasan al-Basri (d. 728), Ibrahim ibn Adham of Balkh (d. *c.* 777), Bibi Rabia of Basra (d. 801), Bayezid Bistami (d. 874), Junaid Baghdadi (910), Mansur Hallaj (d. 922), Ghazali (d. 1111), Abdul Qadir Gilani (d. 1166), and Ibn al-Arabi (d. 1240) and Jili (b. 1365), are some of the important figures in the development of Sufi doctrines. Their voluminous writings address complicated arguments concerning God, the Pure being, devoid of qualities and relations and uncontaminated by the world of phenomena. For example, Jili, in his *Al Insānul Kāmil fī Mārifati al awākhir wa al awāil*, 'The Man Perfect in knowledge of the last and the first things', writes:

> The absolute is the simple essence in which no name or quality or relation is manifested. When any of these appears in it, that idea is referred to that which appears in the Essence, not to the pure Essence, inasmuch as the Essence, by the law of its nature, comprehends universals, particulars, and relations, not as they are judged to exist but as they are judged to be naughted under the might of the transcendental oneness of the essence. (Nicholson 1921: 95)

Early Sufis were persecuted. Zar al-Ghifar (d. 653) was exiled during the reign of Usman (644–56) due to his outspokenness. Abu Darda bin Zaid used to say that one hour of reflection is better than forty nights of ritual prayers. According to Abu Darda, the practice of the principles of Islam and understanding its true essence was better than observing its rituals (Rizvi 1986: 22). This and similar statements upset the orthodox Muslim clergy. They declared that Abu Darda's statement flew directly against the five pillars of Islam, the first of which is the observation of *namaz*. Therefore those who preached blasphemous ideas must be punished. On the persecution of the early Sufis, Rizvi writes, 'Hasan al-Basri's bold criticism of the repressive religio-political policies of Hajjaj bin Yusuf, the Umayyad governor of Iraq, compelled him to go into hiding in 705 where he was forced to remain until Hajjaj's death in 714' (Rizvi 1986: 27). Consequently, many sufis became cautious and either moved to isolated retreats (*khānqāhs*), travelled to other countries in search of safety, or kept a low profile.

Mansur al-Hallaj (b. 858) was a wandering preacher with a large number of disciples. He had travelled through India and Turkistan learning about Buddhism and Manichaeism (Rizvi 1968: 57). After his second pilgrimage to Mecca, he proclaimed that he had experienced a mystic union. He was imprisoned, later tortured and hanged in 922.

> Sufism was an esoteric system, partly because it was continually accused of being heretical, partly because it was held to be incomprehensible and dangerous if expounded to those who had not received the necessary spiritual training. It was handed down within orders of adepts, who were forbidden to reveal the most important tenets of belief (though some occasionally did), from sheikh to pupil. Different sufis living at different times have clearly believed different things, and most sufi authors tend to retreat into paradox at crucial moments, either because they feel their beliefs are genuinely inexpressible by other means or because they fear orthodox reprisal. (Darbandi and Davis 1984: 10)

In time, the ascetic movement[3] became systematized, and the followers of Sufism spread from Basra southeast to Balkh and eventually to north and south India.[4] A number of scholars have studied the philosophy, beliefs, and practices of the various Sufi sects in detail.[5] Certain primary beliefs and practices were common to most Sufi sects. For example, most Sufis believe that one must aspire to subdue the *nafs*, the lower self. According to the Sufis, *nafs* is that component of one's make-up which is responsible for the desire for pleasures of life. For a Sufi, the struggle to control one's lust for material and sensual pleasures is the greatest *jihad*, the true struggle in the service of God. In order to control base desires, the Sufis engage in vigils and strict 'methods' or *tarīqat* to achieve their spiritual goals.

A number of scholars believe that this mystical movement was influenced by early Christian, Zoroastrian, Hindu, and Buddhist philosophies. Sufi masters travelled through diverse regions where they were exposed to a plethora of philosophical systems. Khurasan was then a flourishing centre for new religio-political movements. Hinduism and Buddhism were studied, and Judaism, Christianity, and the Zoroastrianism of the Magi priesthood were also practised throughout the area. The influences of these philosophical systems were manifested in the teaching and practices of the medieval Sufi teachers. For example, it is said that after travelling through India, Mansur al-Hallaj went on his next pilgrimage, 'this time only wearing an Indian loin-cloth round his waist and a piece of patched and motley cloth thrown around his shoulders' (Rizvi 1986: 57).

Some of Hallaj's writings have been translated into French by Louis Massignon. His concepts are said to be identical with those of the leading Christian mystic, St. John of the Cross. 'Jesus was a model of self-denial and of the saintly life. That sufis tended to see Jesus in the light of their own traditions does not lessen the significance of the impact of the Nestorian and Jacobite churches on the movement' (Rizvi 1986: 32).

In his *Studies in Islamic Mysticism*, Reynold Nicholson writes:

> The markedly Christian flavor of the Hallajian doctrine condemned it in Moslem eyes, and while later Sufis develop its main ideas and venerate Hallaj himself as a martyr who was barbarously done to death because he had proclaimed the Truth, they interpret his *Ana al-Haqq* in the light of an idealistic monism which reduces all antitheses—including *lāhūt* and *nāsūt*—to necessarily correlated aspects of the universal Essence. His doctrine in its original form has only recently been recovered and given to the world by Massignon, to whose learned

and brilliant monograph every student of Sufism is deeply indebted. (Nicholson 1921: 80–1)

In tandem with the theory that Sufism was influenced by Christian philosophy, scholars argue that there are a number of common features in the practices of Buddhism and Sufism which clearly demonstrate a strong Buddhist influence on Sufism. Some of these are as follows: Monastic establishments in both belief systems insist on total renunciation of material possessions. Both systems agree that the first step towards eternal bliss is to conquer one's base desires. The two systems invite people to a life of discipline, asceticism, and poverty. Further, Schimmel observes that

The first noted ascetic of the East, Ibrahim ibn Adham, hailed from Balkh, in the ancient province of Bactria. Although he was the scion of Arab settlers, a central motif of the Buddha legend was transferred to him: he becomes in legends the prince who leaves home to wander in homelessness. (Schimmel 1992: 102)

According to Laleh Bakhtiar, Zoroastrianism also influenced Sufism. The twin concepts of law in nature and conflict in Nature contributed to the development of Sufi cosmology (Bakhtiar 1976: 7).

Discussing the interaction between medieval Hindu mystic tradition and Sufism, Athar Abbas Rizvi says:

The study of the interaction between medieval Hindu mystic traditions and sufism has been marred by deep prejudices and studded with conflicting hypotheses. . . . The fact that mystic urges are now recognized as inherent in all religious systems tends to dampen such theories as those expressed by early Western orientalists that sufism developed from an Aryan reaction against the conquering Semitic Arabs. (Rizvi 1986: 322)

Rizvi discusses the similarities the early scholars of Sufism and the Yogis found in their respective systems from the eleventh century onwards in India.

The topics discussed at the *jama at-khana* gatherings of Baba Farid were of great interest to visiting Siddhas whose beliefs were founded on Hatha Yoga. Supplementing these scraps of information is al-Biruni, unquestionably a profound authority on comparative religions, who notes sufi parallels in the *Yoga Sutra* of Patanjali, which he himself translated into Arabic. He also mentions similarities with *Samkhya*, one of the six schools of classical Hindu philosophy, and with the *Bhagavad Gita*.

. . . .

According to al-Biruni the sufi parallel is contained in the following theory: The terms of the sufi as to the *knowing* being and his attaining the *stage of knowledge* come to the same effect, for they maintain that he has two souls—an eternal one, not exposed to change and alternation, by which he knows that which is hidden, the transcendental world, and performs wonders; and another, a human soul, which is liable to being changed and being born. The bodies are the snares of the souls for the purpose of acquiring recompense. He who arrives at the stage of liberation has acquired, in his actual form of existence, the recompense for all the doing of the past. (Rizvi 1986: 324–5)

Many religious systems concur with the theory that life is but a bridge between 'what was' and what 'will be'. One must cross this bridge in the most unencumbered manner possible. A wise man does not overload himself when crossing a bridge because by its very nature a bridge is fragile; nor should he think of building on a bridge. According to the Sufi philosophy, the human soul which finds itself trapped in the human body always yearns for union with its source. For a sufi, life on earth is itself a time of exile. The opening lines of Rumi's *Masnavī* reiterate the soul's mournful longing. Metaphorically, the song of the reed represents the lament of the soul. The soul is likened to a reed which has been plucked away from the reed-bed and has been formed into a musical instrument, just like all souls have a physical form in this life. However, the reed wishes to be reunited to the primary reed-bed. It wails:

Listen to the reed, how it tells a tale, complaining of separations—
Saying, 'Ever since I was parted from the reed-bed, my lament hath caused man and woman to moan.
I want a bosom torn by severance, that I may unfold (to such a one) the pain of love-desire.
Every one who is left far from his source wishes back the time when he was united with it. (Nicholson 1977: 5)

Given the fact that one has no control over the life span one is endowed with, is it possible for a soul to experience union with its source even when it is trapped in a physical form? The answer, according to William Chittick, lies in effort and God's grace. He states:

To undertake the discipline of the path, a man must exert himself to the utmost of his ability. By obeying the law, and striving to please the Eternal Beloved, a man can find divine grace. In the context of Islam, the law is the *Śariah* as laid down in the Quran. Additionally, to follow the example of the Prophet, *Sunnah*, is to follow knowledge. The third dimension of Sufism is to purify the soul so that it may attain spiritual realization. In Sufi literature the heart of the mystic is often compared to a mirror. The reflection of the Divine Beauty is dependent on the clarity of the mirror. The mystic is instructed to work constantly on polishing the mirror of his soul. The act of polishing the mirror of the heart simply means to refrain from all thoughts which may pose an obstacle along the path of spiritual purification. There may be temptations to resist and tests which examine the sincerity of the seeker. The seeker should embrace the path of spiritual realization only if he is willing to sacrifice what is dearest to him including his own life. (Chittick 1983: 160)

Discussing Rumi's theology on the basis of his *Masnavī*, Schimmel writes:

Rumi sees, in accordance with the Sufi terminology, the whole spiritual life as a path, or a ladder; and the same holds true for life in general. There is no rest at any one of the stations:

> Our cry is like the bell in the caravan,
> or like the thunder's voice when the clouds are wandering:
> Oh traveler, do not bind thy heart to any station,
> that you may not become sleepy at the time of attraction.

The call, *ar-rahil*, Start the journey! is often heard in Rumi's poetry; many are called to leave home and family and to set out on the spiritual journey. Only travelling brings everything to perfection; the lean crescent moon grows into a majestic being during his journey, and the sun appears more radiant in the morning after her journey at night. Rain becomes transformed into pearls when they enter into the ocean, and the Prophet's hegira indicates the importance of leaving one's home and gaining a new kingdom on a higher level before returning home again. Matured in separation, the traveller returns home, and the lover who has burnt himself in the flame of suffering, comes back and sees only his waiting friend, no longer himself, so that he is lovingly accepted into the house. Thus every moment of human life is a step along the upward journey which culminates in death—spiritual or corporeal—and then resurrection. The more man proceeds on this path, the deeper his longing to come closer to the mysterious abyss, the higher his ambition to soar to the summit of Mountain Qāf. (Schimmel 1993: 325–6)

According to Schimmel, the Sufi concept of 'journey in God' was elaborated in the Persian *masnavī* tradition even before Rumi. She observes that the theme of the 'journey' was already present in the didactic *masnavīs* of Sanāī and Attār, Rumi's predecessors. Schimmel suggests that perhaps these provided the inspiration to encourage Rūmī's fuller treatment of the theme of journey, as an upward movement of the soul on a spiritual ascent, in his own *Masnavī* (Schimmel 1993: 326). This is a very significant piece of information because it establishes the fact that the Sufi concept of a soul's spiritual journey was already been reflected and elaborated upon in the Persian *masnavī* literary tradition before its adaptation and transformation in the Indo-Sufi *masnavī* genre.

In the subsequent section we shall, along with a general discussion of the various stations (*maqāmāt*) a soul experiences on its mystical journey, take a look at some of the corresponding parallels in the Persian and the Indo-Sufi *masnavīs*.

In his book, *History of Sufism in India*, Rizvi writes:

> Shaikh Najmuddin Kubra believed that the ways of God were as numerous as the breaths of His creatures, but that three ways (those of *akhyar, abrar, shattar*) were pre-eminently superior. The quickest way of all was the *shattar*. There are ten rules for the achievement of the Shattariyya goal: 1) repentance, 2) renunciation of the world, 3) trust in God, 4) contentment, 5) retreat, 6 contemplation of God. 7) patience, 8) satisfaction, 9) *zikr*, and 10) concentrated attention on God. (Rizvi 1983: 156)

In *The Sufi Path of Love: The Spiritual Teachings of Rumi*, Chittick writes:

> Once having entered the way, the disciple begins to undergo a process of inward transformation. If he is among those destined to reach spiritual perfection, he will climb the ascending rungs of a ladder stretching to heaven and beyond'. In the chapter entitled 'The Discipline of the Way' Chittick, in the light of Rumi's works, examines the practices of the Sufis to purify themselves. Chittick also comments upon the role and relationship of the three most important factors necessary, according to the Sufi doctrine, for spiritual purification. These are: a) the ritual prayers, b) the faith, and c) the love for the Eternal Beloved. By constantly observing and diligently adhering to the practices prescribed by the Sufi masters, the soul of the disciple goes through several stages, *maqāmāt*, of gradual spiritual transformation to realize its goals. (Chittick 1983: 13)

The Sufis also believe that the memory of the experiences of these spiritual stations, *maqāmāt*, remains intact within the adept who has travelled the Sufi path of gnosis. It is believed that the path to spiritual realization is like travelling through a dangerous maze. One needs to find the assistance of another traveller who has gone through the stages of spiritual purification and, in the maze of conflicting and confusing lanes, knows the right way to get to the goal. Such a person is a spiritual preceptor, a *pīr* or *shaikh*, equivalent of an Indian *guru*. The significance of the spiritual preceptor cannot be underestimated in the Sufi system. Here is what Rumi says in his *Masnavī*:

> The Pīr is (like) summer, and (other) people are (like) the autumn month; (other) people are like night, and the Pīr is the moon.
> Choose a Pīr, for without a Pīr this journey is exceeding full of woe and affright and danger.
> Without an escort you are bewildered (even) on a road you have travelled many times (before). (Nicholson 1977: 160)

In *Cāndāyan*, Daud sings the praises of his own spiritual preceptor, Shaikh Zainuddin:

> Shaikh Jainadī (Zainuddin) has led me to the path of right conduct, thus all the sins are eliminated. . . . If you can win his heart, your entire family is cleansed (of sins); sins are continually cast off, by serving Jainadī. (M. Gupta 1967: 8)

As discussed above, there are many paths to God, and the sequence of the experiences at the different *maqāmāt* may vary according to the *tarīqat* or the method the Sufi novice selects for himself. However, even before the novice decides to take the path of gnosis, there has to be a spiritual awakening. The first step in the spiritual journey of a soul is to fall in love with Eternal Beauty. Eternal Beauty is an attribute of God and one of the 99 beautiful names, *asma al-husna*. The Koran says, 'Wherever you turn, there is the Face of God (2: 115).' God created the world of phenomena to manifest Himself and when He saw His reflection, He was pleased.[6]

Only if a person is destined to attain spiritual perfection does he undergo the experience of falling in love with the Beloved. In Sufi literature, the earthly beloved is the symbol of the Eternal Beloved. The lover represents the seeking soul; the hardships he encounters and conquers towards fulfilment of his goal are the various stages of progress along the path of his spiritual journey. Love at first sight is often the starting point of the soul on its mystic journey.[7]

In both the Persian and Indo-Sufi *masnavīs*, the first sighting may occur either on the occasion of a face-to-face encounter, by some sign, descriptions, premonitions, or by a friend or bird describing the form and virtues of the beloved. Sometimes the first sight of the beloved is obtained by looking at her picture or seeing her in a dream. Sometimes the lover gets a sign in a dream leading him to her. Love aroused at first sight takes the lover to the next experience, when, he as lover, does not see any other recourse but seek to be united with his beloved.

In the Sufi *masnavī* literature, the beauty of the beloved and her inaccessibility is representative of the attributes of God. The lover represents the yearning soul which is striving to break the bondage of the world of phenomena to reach Eternal Beauty. The worldly beloved is only a symbol of the eternal beloved. Her beauty is a means to lead the mystic to Ultimate Beauty. In his *History of Sufism in India*, Rizvi briefly discusses *Cāndāyan*, specifically the treatment of Cāndā's beauty and what it represents. He also comments on the extent to which *Cāndāyan* could be reconciled with Persian ideas on mysticism by a contemporary scholar, Shaikh Abdul Quddus. Rizvi writes:

> It is interesting that Shaikh Abdul Quddus lectured on the *Chanda'in* with the same intensity as when he lectured on the works of Ibn al-Arabi, Fakhr al-Din Iraqi and Sa'adi. The Persian translation allegorically describes Chanda as a piece of unreachable fruit.
>
> . . .
>
> A fruit is seen in the heavens on a lofty tree.
> Our hands cannot hope to reach it.
> Anyone who is able to extend his hands high,
> How can he touch the branches of that heavenly tree.
> There are lots of people to guard the fruit throughout the day and night.
> He who tries even to look at it is likely to be killed.
>
> The analogy is subtle: Mystics get a glimpse of the Supreme but God Himself is beyond their reach. (Rizvi 1986: 365–6)

Regarding the description of the beauty of Cāndā in a highly stylized genre known as the *nakh-śikh varṇan*, Rizvi writes:

> The *nakh śikh* of the *Chanda'in* made a deep impact on later writers of Hindi *masnawis* and were reproduced chiefly because of the great prestige of its author as a mystic. Shaikh Abdul Quddus, in a letter to Shaikh Jalal Thaneswari on the *Wahdat-al Wujud*, quoted a *doha* from the *Chanda'in* to prove that although lovers sought to meet their beloveds, they were always thwarted. The *doha* is immediately followed by lines from a verse from the Qur'an in which Moses urges God to reveal Himself but his request is rejected on the grounds that it was impossible for Moses to see his Creator. In the Sufi path, *Arani* (show me Yourself) and *Lan Tarani* (you cannot see Me) represented constant conflict between the devotee, who wishes to see the divine vision, and God. In another letter to Shah Muhammad about the spiritual ambitions of holy men, Shaikh Abdul Quddus argued, using for emphasis a *doha* from the *Chanda'in*, that only the spiritually adventurous were real men. (Rizvi 1986: 365)

The following story describes how Sam'an was summoned to search for his love. In the Persian *masnavī*, *The Conference of the Birds*, of Farid ud-Din Attar, Sam'an was a great scholar and a legend in his own time. He had a four-hundred-student strong following. He was known for his piety and regular visits to Mecca. People of his town venerated him. And then, a strange dream began to trouble him, night after night. He dreamed that Mecca was left behind and he was worshipping in Rome. To find the meaning of his dream Sam'an goes to Rome where he sees a Christian girl and, to his great dismay, falls in love with her.

> Love sacked his heart; the girl's bewitching hair
> Twined round his faith impiety's smooth snare.
> The Sheikh exchanged religion's wealth for shame,
>
> A hopeless heart submitted to love's fame.
> 'I have no faith,' he cried. 'The heart I gave
> Is useless now; I am the Christian's slave.
>
> (Darbandi and Davis 1984: 59)

Sam'an finds himself in an unfamiliar surrounding, among stranger people who followed a different religion. To them he is a stranger without wealth or resources. At this moment in his life Sam'an, the lover, finds himself on uncertain ground. He has left home and the comforts associated with home. After seeing the beloved, he cannot turn back. He must now find a way to reach her. He faces difficulties and humiliation at each step. In the long ordeal of his quest his old identity fades away and his pride in himself is lost. He becomes a different man. Finally, his sacrifices and commitment bear fruit and Sam'an and his beloved are united in spirit.

Interestingly there is a parallel to this in *Saundarānanda*, Aśvaghoṣa's narrative in Sanskrit. The story in brief is as follows: Nanda, Gautama's half brother, lives comfortably in his palace with his lovely wife Sundarī. However, he is destined to receive divine blessings, so the Buddha himself visits Nanda's home at a moment when everybody is busy. When Nanda finds out that the Buddha did not receive the honour due to him, he is horrified and ashamed. He rushes out of his palace in search of Buddha so as to cajole him back into the palace and show him appropriate hospitality.

However, some time passes before Nanda gets a chance to speak to his brother. During one of their discourses, Buddha takes Nanda on a journey to the celestial lands where Nanda is captivated by a nymph. Now he has no desire to go back to the comforts of his palace anymore. In the hopes of finding the beloved, Nanda voluntarily practices austerities. Once Nanda chooses to become a novice, it is by way of the transformation he experiences in the course of his spiritual journey that he understands the meaning of the world of phenomena and is ultimately able to discriminate between form and essence.[8]

These stories share certain common features. Both Nanda and Sam'an belong to the elite and enjoy a life of affluence and comfort in the beginning. Their departure from home is spontaneous. As soon as they step out, they break their connection with the past. Both of them experience disorientation, a life of austerities, and poverty. In a world very different from the one they were used to, both fall in love. Their commitment to their pursuit results in transformation of character. In the end, both achieve spiritual calm. In other words, in the process of spiritual transformation, the icons with which they had first fallen in love are left far behind. The pursuit of physical love is transcended in the enjoyment of a unity of essences. A comparative study of these two stories in conjunction with the storyline of *Cāndāyan* offers an interesting triptych.

Rumi has nothing but pity and disdain for those who look at the world around and within themselves and do not understand that what they are seeing is a veil over reality. The world is a dream, a prison, a trap, foam thrown up from the ocean, dust kicked up by a passing horse. But it is not what it appears to be. If everything that appears to us were just as it appears, the Prophet, who was endowed with such penetrating vision, both illuminated and illuminating, would never have cried out, 'Oh Lord, show us things as they are!' According to Rumi the form is the outward appearance and the essence is the reality which is known to God alone:

> Know that the outward form passes away, but the World of Meaning remains forever.
> How long will you make love with the shape of the Jug? Leave aside the jug's shape: Go seek water!
> Having seen the form, you are unaware of the meaning.
> If you are wise, pick out the pearl from the shell. (Chittick 1983: 18–22)

In other words, attraction for the beauty of form is merely the first step. If the novice believes that he will be successful in his aspirations and pursues his goals unconditionally, the stage of spiritual awakening can lead him through different stations to the Eternal Beauty. As in the above narratives, in *Cāndāyan*, when the hero sees Cāndā for the first time, he loses his appetite for worldly pleasures. He leaves home and practices austerities to find her. Thus we see that spiritual awakening leads the novice to seclusion and a pure way of life. He now prefers to stay away from the comforts and sophistication of an artificial life. He believes that material poverty, *faqīrī*, must be practised. He chooses solitude over the daily humdrum of his earlier existence. This period during which the novice retreats to a secluded place, meditates, repents his sins, contemplates the mercy of God, and longs for union with Eternal Beauty, is known among the Sufis as *khalwat*.

The mainstay of the stage of *khalwat* is faith. The novice must believe that his efforts are being watched and that his sufferings will be rewarded; each of the subsequent stages will lead the disciple to the next; eventually he will reach the stage of gnosis or self-realization. His passion to reach his goal will help him through the difficulties of his journey.[9] The spiritual master is the source of succour at this trying time.

The shaikh, just like a guru, gives the disciple a mantra or prayer formula, which he has to chant constantly.[10] This set of words, when repeated in sequence, will assist the disciple and save him from failing at the most crucial moments of his spiritual journey. Therefore in a Sufi *silsilah* or the chain of adepts, the selection of the spiritual teacher is extremely important. The disciple must have unshakeable faith in the teacher's ability to guide him to gnosis. By the same token the teacher has to be deeply committed to overseeing the novice's progress in his spiritual quest.

The process of repeating God's names, chanting prayers and contemplating the virtues of God is known as *zikr*, which simply means mentioning. Sometimes it is also referred to as 'meditating' or 'remembrance'. Chittick describes it as follows:

> The Sufis do not limit themselves to the ritual prayers and those elements of the Prophet's Sunnah codified in the *Sharī'ah*. They emphasize a deeper understanding of the meaning of the ritual, as opposed to its form; and they add other practices recommended by the *Koran* and the Prophet but not made incumbent upon all believers. In this connection the fundamental Sufi practice, for Rumi as for all Sufi masters, is the 'remembrance' (*dhikr, yād*) of God, which is urged in numerous Koranic verses and prophetic sayings. (Chittick 1983: 150)

In *A History of Sufism in India*, Rizvi Writes:

> Breath control, according to Shaikh Bahauddin, was indispensable for rendering *zikr* effective. Before commencing it the neophyte should choose a clean place and should purify both his outer and inner selves. He need not use *zikr* only with Arabic or Persian words, but could also use a Hindi *zikr*. Shaikh Bahauddin also recommended the sitting posture of *jogis* (Rizvi 1983: 156).

Once the disciple has decided to sacrifice everything that is dear to him in order to achieve his goal and believes that eventually he will find what he is looking for, he has arrived at the stage called *zikr*. At this stage, the disciple must constantly focus on the Beloved, *fikr*, and chanting her names, *zikr*. In a Sufi monastery, often the disciple is asked to move to a secluded place where he is required to meditate. He is either given a set of names selected from the ninety-nine beautiful names of God or a prayer from the Koran as formulae to repeat constantly. However, the novice must contemplate and meditate simultaneously. *Zikr*, the outward expression, and *fikr*, the inner contemplation, must accompany each other.

In literature, the practice and experience of *zikr* by the lover is reflected in a very similar way. For example, elaborating on the practice of *zikr*, Rumi writes:

> His name is the spirit of spirits, His invocation the ruby of mines. His love is in the soul, He is both our refuge and our hope. When I mention His name, good fortune arrives; then the Name becomes the Named, without duality, without hesitation. (Chittick 1983: 158)

In Daud's *Cāndāyan*, when Lorik sees Cāndā for the first time, he becomes unconscious and is taken home on a stretcher. Subsequently, he moves to a deserted shrine in the woods and practices austerities for a year. Cāndā comes to know of Lorik's love for her and sends her maid to visit him. When the maid returns, Cāndā asks her maid about Lorik's condition. The maid replies:

नैन रगत झर दिन असरारू।
भुगुति न जानइ नींद अहारु।
मलिन काम बेधा न संभारइं।
चांद चांद निसि ठाढ पुकारइ। (M. Gupta 1967: 179).

Blood drips from his eyes all day, from secret emotion;
He does not know what sleep is, nor potion;
Unsustained, pierced with love, he is stained;
Cāndā, Cāndā, he stands, calling through the night.

Chanting or repeating certain words or phrases again and again is universal to most religions of the world. As in the case of many other religions, Sufis believe that *zikr* lifts you to a different plane of consciousness. Man must have faith in God's infinite mercy and grace and expect compassion from Him alone. Rumi says:

> Keep your aspiration high, for if you keep it low, the King's chamberlain will drive you away—'Begone!' Everyone sees the Unseen in proportion to the

clarity of his heart, and that depends upon how much he has polished it. Whoever has polished it more sees more—more Unseen forms become manifest to him. A man shall have to his account only as he has laboured. (Chittick 1983: 162)

In *Cāndāyan*, when Cāndā succumbs to a snakebite and dies, Lorik is beside himself with grief. He takes it that Cāndā is lost to him due to his own conduct. Still he keeps up his aspirations. Repenting for his sins over and over, Lorik pleads for God's help. To have complete faith in God's compassion is of crucial importance for the novice who embarks on a spiritual odyssey. This stage, when a Sufi expects mercy from God alone, is called *tawakkul*. There comes a point in Lorik's lamentations when he wishes to die in order to be with Cāndā in the life hereafter. This is a pivotal point when Lorik has conquered his love for Cāndā's physical form. He realizes that it is a union of spirits which is fulfilling and gratifying. But it is necessary to get rid of the physical form in order to achieve spiritual union. The physical form represents the human ego or 'selfhood'. For a Sufi, the experience of *fana*, of nullifying the ego, is essential for a true and thoroughgoing spiritual realization that everything he is derives absolutely from God. *Fanā* is the last and highest of the rungs or stages in the spiritual journey of a Sufi.[11] Rumi says:

No one will find his way to the Court of Magnificence until he is annihilated. You are your own shadow—become annihilated in the rays of the Sun! How long will you look at your shadow? Look also at His Light! (Chittick 1983: 179)

At this point in the *masnavī*, a Gāruḍī happens to come along and brings Cāndā back to life. Expressing his firm belief that his prayers were answered, Lorik says,

अलख निरन्जन जाहि जियावहि। दइअ क लिखा सो मानुस पावइ।

(By the grace of) Alakh Niranjan, (Cāndā) has revived!
A man obtains (joy, when it is so) ordained by divine decree.

Chittick says:

The most common image Rumi employs in speaking of annihilation and naughting the self is that of death. He often quotes the Prophet's advice, 'Die before you die!' and he likes to refer to the verse of the famous Sufi martyr Hallāj: 'Kill me, my faithful friends! For in my slaughter in my life—my death is in my life and my life in my death'. (Chhitick 1983: 183)

Discussing the spiritual station of *fana*, Schimmel writes that 'dying through love involves resurrection on a higher plane. In Rumi's lyrics we find wonderful descriptions of the state of man, who, after leaving this world, will experience true union and endless meetings with the Beloved. Therefore, why should a man fear death?' (Schimmel 1993: 325). Narrating one of the incidents in Rumi's life, Schimmel writes that when his friend Zarkub died and was buried, Rumi celebrated his death with a *samā*, a mystical dance accompanied by drums and flute—because death is not a separation but, as the dervishes say, according to Schimmel, an '*ors*, a spiritual wedding. However, events like a *samā* after a funeral must have shocked the orthodox circles of the population' (Schimmel 1993: 27).

In the Indo-Sufi *masnavīs*, the concept of *ors*, spiritual union, is figuratively expressed as the physical union of the hero and the heroine. However, this concept was not easily accepted by all Muslims. According to Schimmel,

> In ancient strata of religion, sexual union was conceived as a symbol for spiritual union, and even the *Upaniṣadas*, abstract as their teachings may sound in many places, describe the highest bliss as comparable to being embraced by a beloved wife, but as the normative theologians disliked the ecstatic dance as a means to 'union', they also objected to a terminology in which 'love' was the central concept. . . . The theological discussions about the terminology of 'Love' continued for a long time in the ninth and tenth centuries, long before the thought of a human being as a target of one's love appeared in Sufism—a love which, to be sure, was never to be fulfilled but remained (or at least was supposed to remain) chaste and spiritual. The mystics then became aware that 'the metaphor is the bridge to Reality' and that love of a beautiful human being was, as they say *ishq majāzī*, 'metaphorical love', which would lead to *ishq haqīqī*, 'true love' of the only One who was worthy of love. (Schimmel: 1994: 105)

In conclusion, the mystic journey of a Sufi is reflected in the *masnavī* genre in a number of ways and the various stations of the spiritual journey are elaborated in detail. Once a soul experiences awakening, provided it is steadfast in its quest, it progresses through a number of spiritual stations. In the process, there is a change in the psyche. The last and the highest stage of the spiritual journey is called *fanā*. It signifies a total transformation as the soul attains self-realization through its annihilation in the Unity of Being.

Generally speaking, the theme of a journey, a metaphor for a soul's spiritual ascent, is basic to all *masnavī* genres. As for the basic *masnavī* plot, its skeletal form is quite predictable. Why should we then look at the *masnavī* corpus, if all the stories are more or less the same? I would like to compare the craft of the author of a *masnavī* to a musician trained in Indian classical music tradition. All he has to work with is a basic framework of notes which should remain in a certain order in the ascending and descending scales. It is up to the musician to develop and improvise within this framework. With his creativity and imagination, he imbues these few simple notes with body and soul. As a result, no two interpretations of a *rāga* ever sound exactly the same. By the same token, each *masnavī* is worth of reading and is unique in its own right.[12]

NOTES

1. Rizvi's *History of Sufism in India* is a trailblazing study of Sufism. The work of Chittick, Ernst, Falconer, Schimmel, Haeri, Bakhtair, Nicholson and Arberry is also noteworthy.
2. See A. Schimmel 1992: 101; A.J. Arberry 1992: 17; S.A. Rizvi 1986: 28; and C.B. Pandey 1966: 7.
3. See Rizvi 1986: 1–18.
4. See B. Behari 1962: 97–176; Rizvi 1986: 405–9; and M. Mujeeb 1985: 160–7.
5. See Nicholson, Arberry, Schimmel, Chittick and Ernst. Works of many great Sufis such as Imam Ghazali, Ibd al-Arabi and Huzviri have also been translated into European languages.
6. Browne 1902: 440.
7. This topic is discussed in detail in Embree 1988: 454–8.
8. See 'Pitfalls of the Path' in Chittick 1983: 289–90. Also Pandey's discussion of the allegorical interpretation of Cāndā's beauty in S.M. Pandey 1968: 1–26.
9. Talat Halman, 'Jalāl al-Din Rumi: Passions of the Mystic Mind', in *Persian Literature*, ed. Ehsan Yarshater.
10. See Rizvi's discussion of the invocation of God's names in his *History of Sufism in India*, p. 156.
11. 'Annihilation in God', vol. 1, Browne 1902: 443.
12. For a discussion of 'Never-Repeating Self-Disclosures', see Chittick's *Sufi Path of Knowledge*, p. 103.

5

Two Episodes from *Cāndāyan:* Interpretation and Exegesis

In this chapter I shall elaborate on my analysis of the allegorical aspect of Indo-Sufi literature by providing detailed interpretations of two sections of *Cāndāyan*, the 'snakebite' episode, and the 'homecoming'. These sections particularly lend themselves to the exegesis of the Indo-Sufi *masnavī* genre in terms of its Sufi contents. When the symbolism of the text is held up for examination, each section unfolds spontaneously to reveal its superficial as well as its quintessential meaning.

The Snakebite Episodes

The two snakebite episodes occur in quick succession. If a writer wants to re-visit an interesting feature, a suitable interval must be allowed to pass before doing so. However, this does not happen in *Cāndāyan*. I examine the allegorical aspect of the text and suggest a reason why these episodes had to be placed back to back. My aim is to demonstrate that actually in the juxtaposition of the two snakebite episodes of the *Cāndāyan*, the entire concept of a Sufi's mystic journey is encapsulated.

In P. Gupta's edition of *Cāndāyan*, published in 1984, the two snakebite episodes begin with stanza 333 and end with stanza 360. The first occurs when Lorik is eloping with Cāndā. He heads towards a place called Hardī Pāṭan in the Kalinga region where he hopes to visit some kinsmen. On the way they halt at a brahmin's house for the night. Here, in the course of the night, Cāndā is bitten by a snake and dies. Later, she is revived by a *guṇī's* or *gāruḍī's* mantras. Lorik offers the ornaments of his wrists and arms to the *gāruḍī*, but the *gāruḍī* asks for *all* of Lorik's ornaments and takes them away with him.

The second snakebite episode occurs when Cāndā and Lorik resume their journey the next day. When night falls, they take shelter under a large tree. Here, once again, Cāndā succumbs to a fatal snakebite. For two days and a night, Lorik cries in anguish for Cāndā. He weeps, laments, and recalls the various risks they took to be with each other. He describes how miserably hopeless it is for him to be without Cāndā. He blames himself for the tragic incident and repents his sins. Finally, he comes to the decision that he cannot live without Cāndā and decides to immolate himself on her funeral pyre, holding her in an embrace. With this plan in mind, he begins to cut wood. However, another *guṇī* comes along and Lorik implores him to revive Cāndā. In return, he pledges all his belongings and promises to serve the *guṇī* for as long as he lives and also in the next life. Once again Cāndā is brought back to life and they continue on their journey.

Why did Daud choose to have two snakebite episodes instead of one? And why are they placed one right after the other? Mataprasad Gupta and Parmeshwarilal Gupta both agree that the second snakebite episode is entirely Maulana Daud's creation and that the original folk tale of Mainā-Lorik had only one.

My explanation is that when Daud composed *Cāndāyan*, he selected the folktale of Canaini, merely as a point of reference. The changes he brought into the story and the sophisticated poetic form he gave it altered the focus. He transformed a simple entertaining folk tale into an elevated literary work and a vehicle for transmitting Sufi doctrines. The journey of Lorik is essentially a journey of the individual self in search of the Universal Self, and the two snakebite episodes highlight a crucial point in this quest. Lorik arrives at the high mark of his spiritual journey at this time.

Daud created the second snakebite episode as a facilitating incident to allow Lorik to continue on his mystic journey. Once Lorik recognizes his goal and sets off on his quest, he arrives at the pinnacle of his quest only in the second snakebite episode. Therefore, if Daud had not used the second snakebite episode to complete the symbolic journey of the mystic Lorik, his *masnavī* would have remained an entertaining love narrative or *Hindī premākhyān*. Let us see why the second episode was essential for moving the emphasis from entertainment to an exposition of Sufi doctrine. Since a *masnavī* by definition, is an allegorical mystical poem, the story and its purpose must be understood on a different level and the Sufi symbols must be closely examined.

Cāndā is the symbol of Divine Majesty and Glory. In some of the oral versions of *Cāndāyan*, the name of the hero is Nūrak, derived from the Arabic word *nūr*, light.[1] It is important to notice that the names of the hero and heroine both embody two sources of light. Light plays a very significant role in virtually all religious belief systems. In the context of human life, darkness is the symbol of intellectual ignorance and spiritual slumber and light represents the end of that state. Discussing the important role of light in the Islamic tradition, Annemarie Schimmel writes that the Prophet Muhammad prayed for more light in his sight and perception.[2]

The moon is a source of light and beauty in the firmament. But more importantly, the light of the moon is at best the reflection of the supreme source of light that endows it with light and beauty, namely, the sun. Therefore, princess Cāndā is the reflection as well as the representation of divine brilliance. Ultimately all worldly beauty and light is reflection of the Divine Glory. The human soul is likened to a mirror which reflects the light emanating from its eternal source. The Koran says: *Allahu Nur al samewati wa al arz*, i.e., 'God is the light of the firmaments and the earth (24: 45).' The more a Sufi works towards purifying and cleansing the mirror of his soul, the better prepared he is to receive the divine light.[3] Once a thirst for eternal beauty has been awakened, the first step a Sufi must take towards his mystical journey is in the direction of the *maqam-i-khalwat*, a place of retreat and vigil. Concerning the importance of this first step, Laleh Bakhtiar says:

> The premise or logic behind entering *khalwat*, the gateway to the subsequent stages of the mystical journey, is that respite from the daily routines and distance from one's immediate surroundings provide the seeker with a different perspective (Bakhtiar 1976: 94)

In both snakebite episodes, Lorik is away from the two places he is most preoccupied with, his home and the battlefield. In the first episode, he is at a Brahmin's place and in the second, he is beneath a large tree. Here an association with the 'tree of knowledge'[4] comes to mind as do other images, as for example that of the account of the Buddha's enlightenment.[5]

According to the Sufis, 'If entered into and embraced with sincerity, the stage of the spiritual retreat has the potential to open up the door to the next stage of the mystic journey' (Mir Valiuddin 1987: 152). Defining the spiritual stations of the internal experiences in Sufism, Carl Ernst writes, 'The Sufi Sarraj gives the meaning of stations as: "the station of the creatures before God, in terms of where one stands from devotions, exertions, meditations, and concentrating on God. Repentance (*tawba*), asceticism (*zuhd*), poverty (*faqr*), patience (*sabr*), trust in God (*tawakkul*) and satisfaction (*rida*) are *some* of the principal stations' (Ernst 1992: 10).

A novice must practice austerities. In order to do so, one must give up the life of worldly luxuries and comforts. This is the stage of renunciation, *faqr*. The novice must find a secluded place where he can meditate. When he chooses to live the life of a hermit, he goes to a *khalwat*. His experience of asceticism is *zuhd*. In his retreat, the novice meditates and repeats the names of God. The act of mentioning God's name again and again, 'remembrance', is called *zikr*. The act of chanting a single word or a formula of prayers is a part of 'remembrance'. The novice repents for his sins. The asking for forgiveness and repenting for one's sins is *tawba*. The seeker pursues his goals with patience, *sabr*, and bows down to the will of God. His unconditional acceptance of the will of God is *rida*. Peaceful acceptance of the will of God is also a basic tenet of Islam, as encapsulated in its own name. Additionally, the novice believes in the mercy and compassion of God and expects that God will respond. This experience is the state of *tawakkul*. The final state in a mystic's spiritual journey is *fanā*, the complete annihilation of ego.

In the light of the this brief explanation, it is desirable to briefly trace Lorik's journey through a few of the above-mentioned stations: The first step a Sufi novice has to take is to disengage himself from his daily routine life and go to a place where he can be alone and undisturbed to practice meditation. The place of solitude is called *khalwat*. Sufi *khānqāhs* or seminaries have a special place for retreat for the purpose of meditation. Repentance, *tawba*, is the next station: In the snakebite episodes, Lorik repents for his sins again and again and blames only himself for his predicament. He does not blame anyone else. On the contrary, he says, he got what he deserved:

जस कीन्हेउं, जस पायउं (M. Gupta 1967: 316)

I reap what I sowed.

Asceticism, *zuhd*, is the next station Lorik experiences. Comparing his condition to Rāma's when he was living an ascetic's life in Pancavaṭī, Lorik says that he, too is enduring Rāma's ordeal, लोरहिं राम अवस्था परी (M. Gupta 1967: 320).

Poverty, *faqr*, is considered a very important state for a Sufi to embrace. This is Lorik's next stop. When he arrives there during the first and second snakebite episodes, he gives away all his material possessions and is willing to serve the *gāruḍī* all his life and into the next. Lorik says:

हाथ क मुंदरी, खरग कटारा, कान क कुन्डर, चांद गियं हारा।
अउर जो सांठि गांठि हइ मोरी, देहौ सभ बलिहारई तोरी।
तोरै गुनहिं चांद जउ लहउं। दुहौ जरम चेर होइ रहउं।। (M. Gupta 1967: 326)

The ring on my finger, the scimitar and the dagger,
The necklace on Cānd's neck, the earrings in her ear . . .
In addition, what ever the assets in my pocket
or be it the capital in my purse,
I shall give you all, I devoutely swear,
If only I get Cānd back with your prayers.
In both lives, this and the next,
I'll remain your humble servant.

From the story we know that the *gāruḍī* was successful in bringing Cāndā back to life with his mantras. However, having lost all his wealth, Lorik is forced to become a *faqīr*.

The next *maqāmāt* Lorik comes to are the stations of patience, *sabr*, and mystical trust in God, *tawakkul*. The novice must reconcile himself with his share. In fact a human being's complete acceptance and bowing to the will of God is the essence of Islam, as already mentioned. A Sufi accepts what comes to him and expects mercy from God alone. After Cāndā succumbs to a snakebite the second time, Lorik laments bitterly and says:

दया गुसाई सिरजनहारा, तोहि छाडि कस करउं पुकारा (M. Gupta 1967: 316)

O my maker, have mercy, my Lord.
Except you, who (else) should I call upon?

When a sufi novice enters *maqam-i-khalwat*, he undertakes to engage in constant *zikr*. During both snakebite episodes, Lorik recalls the radiance of the joy he had in Cāndā's company and repeats her name over and over again:

संग न साथी, भें भें रोवा, मीत जो होत, से दई बिछोवा।
कर गहि, चांद चांद गुहरावइ, धुनि धुनि सीस नारि पै लावई। (M. Gupta 1967: 322)

Deprived of his companion, Lorik wept aloud shamelessly;
He held Cāndā's arm while calling out to her repeatedly.

He leaned over Cāndā's body
And beat his head over and over again.

Constant remembrance of God and chanting His many names helps a disciple disengage from his immediate surroundings. He moves from the level of 'self' to concentrate on the 'divine'. Rumi illustrates this point in his *Masnavī* with a story entitled 'The story of the person who knocked at a friend's door'. His friend from within asked who he was; he said, 'Tis I' and the friend answered, 'Since thou art thou, I will not open the door: I know not any friend that is "I" ' (Nicholson 1977: 167).

A summary of the story is as follows. A man falls in love with a beauty. He wants to see her and so approaches her abode and knocks at the door. The person within asks, 'Who is it?' 'It is I', comes the reply. 'Turn away, it is not the right time to see the one you seek', says the person from within. The lover leaves and returns at a different time. However, the same incident is repeated and he has to leave. In this way, the lover visits the house of the beloved over and over again. One day, when the lover knocks at the entrance, from within comes the same question, 'Who is there?' From the lover comes the answer, 'You, it is you.' 'Enter now', comes the command from within.

Towards the close of the second snakebite episode, Lorik actually arrives at the stage where he can distinguish between the essence and the mirror that reflects the divine reality. When Cāndā dies from the second snakebite, a considerable amount of time passes during which Lorik meditates on his past life, calls for help, and realizes the nature of true love (M. Gupta 1967: 325).

After a day and the second night have passed and the eclipsed moon did not regain its light, Lorik prepares a funeral pyre and, as he holds Cāndā to his chest and prepares to go on the funeral pyre, he proclaims:

भई बात अब जानेउं चांदा, तोरै करन निदान।
जो जिउ जाइ कया कस देखहि, मैं का करब अबान। (M. Gupta 1967: 315)

Only after your demise, Cāndā, have I realized,
If life departs, it is impossible for the form
To remain intact. I have no say in this matter,
Nor is there any other recourse.

Lorik is now prepared to make the ultimate sacrifice, the sacrifice of his own self or ego. At this moment, Lorik is without carnal desires and his mind is pure. In actively embracing self-annihilation, the ultimate sacrifice, he is actually moving towards his goal of union with Eternal Joy and Everlasting life, *fanā*.[6] *Fanā*, the phenomenon of 'naughting the self', is essentially the result of true love, already tested by sacrifice (Chittick 1983: 173).

What is true love and how can one recognize it? It is this question which echoes in many religious traditions and continues to intrigue humankind. There are many Sufi stories which attempt to address this question. Sometimes these stories take the form of parables and sometimes the answer is given directly. Most of the time its a matter of personal communications passed on orally among contemporary Sufis. One such story goes as follows. A Sufi master, Janab Ameer Ali, was once asked: 'How may the true love be recognized and identified?' The teacher replied:

मुहब्बत तो कुरबानियां चाहती है, तहे तेग पेशानियां चाहती है।
जो डर जाए राहे वफा में, मेरी जां, कोई और शै है, मुहब्बत नहीं है।।

Really (it is not very difficult to recognize love because)
 love demands many sacrifices.
Love wishes to put the heads (of the lovers)
Under the scimitar. Then, my dear,
That which trembles in fear, (and shies away from the test of self-sacrifice, i.e., does not give proof of total commitment), is surely something other than true love.

Elaborating on the subject of the mystic journey through various stations, Laleh Bakhtiar writes:

The spiritual stations are degrees of ascent, reached through certain rites and certain difficulties. They are permanent acquisitions, as opposed to states, which are gratuitous gifts that come and go with the attraction of the Divine. (This is the basic difference between *hal*, plural *ahwal* and *maqam*, plural *maqamat*.) The ultimate station, *fanā* is reached when the seeker looses his self in The Self. His final orientation is towards total receptivity: spiritual death. One of the most famous sayings of the Prophet, peace be upon him is 'Die before you die'. The tomb room in Konya of Jalal-al Din Rumi, the founder of the Maulawi Order, is actually the place of his wedding, for the night of his death is celebrated with all the joy that surrounds a wedding. The *urs* or the wedding of the Sufi saints all over the world is actually their death anniversaries celebrated as the day of their annihilation, *fanā*, in the Unity of Being, *wahdat al wajud*. (Bakhtiar 1976: 52)

Once again, the success of the individual soul in attaining union with the Universal Soul lies in the seriousness of pursuit and in complete commitment and readiness to sacrifice. Sacrifice, then, is the key to *fanā*.[7] A *sakhi* attributed to the poet saint Kabīr says:

> जिन ढूंढा तिन पाइयां, गहरे पानी पैठि।
> मैं बूढा, बूडन डरा, रहा किनारे बैठि।। (Tiwari et al. 1985: 490).

> Only those who sink deep into the sea find what they seek;
> Frail and scared of drowning, I remain sitting on the beach.

The presence of the *gāruḍī* or *guṇī* in both the snakebite episodes, and the brahmin's presence in the first, symbolizing the spiritual guide or *hadi*, should also be recognized at this point.[8] In Sufism, the *murśidī-murīdī* relationship is of great significance, because without the guidance of the teacher it would be difficult for the mystic to realize his ultimate goal.

In both episodes, snakebite occurs late at night or, rather, when the day is about to break, as indicated in *kaḍvak* 313 (M. Gupta 1967), पाछिली राति होत भिनुसारा. This time is considered auspicious in many traditions. Symbolically, the veil of darkness or ignorance is about to be lifted and the light of knowledge is beginning to shine. The Koran says '*Allahu Nur al Samawat-i wa al Arz*, God is the light of the firmament and the earth.'

Regarding the question of the two snakebite episodes having been arranged back to back, my explanation is as follows. In the mystic journey the seeker has to move from one stage to the next without a major break. It is of crucial importance that the *maqāmāt* the Sufi novice experiences follow each other closely without a gap. According to Laleh Bakhtiar, when a novice leaves the *khalwat*, his position within the *maqāmāt* can remain effective only on condition that he continue to practise *zikr* (Bakhtiar 1976: 94). Schimmel says, 'In the uninterrupted struggle against the *nafs*, not only are poverty and fasting, nightly vigils and, often, silence required, but also constant introspection' (Schimmel 1992: 104). The key words in the above statements are 'continuation', 'uninterrupted', and 'constant'.

The first snakebite, therefore, is symbolic of Lorik's setting forth on his spiritual journey and his arrival at that particular *maqām* where he offers all his material possessions. Subsequent stations are symbolized in the second snakebite episode where Lorik willingly relinquishes his desire to live in exchange for the eternal happiness he seeks in death. The second episode, therefore, is but a means of uninterrupted and constant continuation and culmination of his spiritual journey.

Only by considering the two snakebite episodes in sequence can we watch Lorik progress successfully through all the prescribed stages on his mystic journey. When he first faces separation from Cāndā, he is distraught.

लोरक बीर बहु कारन करई।
चाहि कपारै कुन्त दै मरई।। (M. Gupta 1967: 310)

Brave Lorik bemoaned and wept;
Taking an ax to his head he wished to die.

Then taking the vow of poverty he gladly gives up all his worldly belongings in order to get Cāndā back: कर कंगन अभरन सभ दीन्हा (M. Gupta 1967: 312). But when he loses Cāndā the second time, he wishes not to continue to live without her. Realizing the nature of true love, Lorik says:

कवनिहु भान्ति न छुटत देखेउं, तेहि रे पिरम कइ झेल।
पिरम खेल सोइ पइ खेलइ सो सिर सतीं खेल।। (M. Gupta 1967: 324)

Those who sustain the wounds of love
Are never seen to escape.
Only those who are willing to wager their heads
Should dare play the game of love.

Actually there is a significant break after these two snakebite episodes. The composer-narrator stops here for a moment and allows Maulana Nathan, who is listening to the story, to step into the narrative and express his opinion. The *kaḍvak* after the snakebite episodes opens with the following rubric in Persian prose: आखिर बिसहर खन्ड चन्द सुखन फरमूदने मौलाना नत्थन, which means, the end of the snake(bite) episode: Maulana Nathan's statement (M. Gupta 1967: 329).

In the exchange between Nathan and Daud, Nathan says, 'Daud sang this song and whoever heard it was visibly moved, जें रे सुना सो गा मुरझाई. Blessed are the words and blessed is the author, and blessed are those who recite it and those who mull and contemplate over its real meaning, धनि रे सबद, धनि लेखनहारा, धनि ते बोल धनि अरथ बिचारा।' (M. Gupta 1967: 329).

To this praise, Daud modestly responds: तोर कहा मैं यह खन्ड गावउं (Ibid. 329), upon your request, I sing this part (of the tale). He proceeds to say that he is reciting, in verse form, the story of Cāndā who was going to Hardi and was bitten by a snake. Daud emphasizes that he has merely repeated the story. In the courtly manner expected of Daud, he credits Nathan for his own accomplishments: Really, it is Nathan who brings forth the tragic emotion, Daud says. 'नथन मलिक दुख बात उभारी।' (M. Gupta 1967: 329). Daud then politely concludes the conversation with the following promise to Nathan: 'In deference to your wish, I shall compose more poems, contemplating deeply in my mind. I bow my head and join my hands in supplication.'

After this exchange, the narrative continues much along the established path of the folktale. For example, the next stanza begins with the following rubric: रवानह शुदन लोरिक व चांदा व रसीदन नजदीक हरदीं, i.e. Lorik and Cāndā set forth and arrive close to Hardī. But somehow, the reader is left with the impression that after Nathan has gone off, the narrator felt he had already arrived at the end of his story. However, he continues for the benefit of the rest of the audience. He almost seems to be saying to the audience still waiting to hear more, 'and so where was I?, Oh, yes, and then. . . .'

Perhaps the truth is that Daud, Nathan and those who are initiated, informed and experienced, quickly grasped the mystic meaning of the snakebite episodes and for them the story had already come to a successful conclusion. But to the uninitiated, the true understanding of the divine can never be logically explained, even with symbols and representations. According to those who have attained the station of knowledge, who are wise and learned, a person experiences and interprets the spiritual phenomenon according to his own purity of mind and depth of understanding. The mirror can only show what it is capable of reflecting. The picture the mirror projects depends totally on how murky or how clean the mirror itself is. Ghalib, in the opening ghazal of his *Diwan*, anthology, says:

आगही दामे शुनीदन जिस तरह चाहे बिछाए,
मुद्दआ अन्का है अपने आलमे तकरीर का (Ghalib, 1st ghazal: 4th couplet).

> No matter how precisely universe of discourse may spread her trap of precedence, to understand the true meaning of (my world of expression) with logic alone, is like capturing the *ankā* (the legendary phoenix), i.e., quite impossible.

The Homecoming Episode

In the *Gṛha Āgaman khaṇḍ* or the 'homecoming episode' Lorik and Cāndā return home to his village, Govar. Mainā, Lorik's wife, has suffered through the entire year of his absence. Once again, there is a conflict between Mainā and Cāndā. However, Lorik pacifies Mainā and brings harmony to his family life.

The Sufi symbols deployed in this concluding chapter need to be closely examined. Why we need to examine symbols and representation when we are reading a *masnavī*, poses an interesting question. The reason is as follows: By definition, the *masnavī* is a literary genre in which a long story is narrated in a designated meter. It often is an allegorical romance, a tale of love, quest, adventure, suffering and subsequent transformation. Often there is a one-to-one symbolic correspondence between certain mystical themes, and the characters and elements of the story. In *Cāndāyan* Lorik represents the soul in quest of the Cosmic Soul represented by Cāndā.

From the Sufi point of view, the role of *Cāndāyan* is far more significant than the role of a *premākhyān*. It is true that *Cāndāyan* has all the spicy elements to keep the layman entertained, and does incorporate almost all the nine *rasas*. However, only when it is examined as a Sufi allegory, does it rise above the definitions of a *premākhyān* and prove to be a vehicle for expanding Sufi doctrine to transport to uninitiated audiences. When we come with him to the last episode, we realize that Lorik has completed his training and has achieved his spiritual goals.

The last chapter of *Cāndāyan* is exclusively devoted to the ultimate essence of the didactic aspects of the story: only after reading the homecoming episode do we realize that Daud was not interested in merely telling an entertaining tale. He had a mission to teach the layman a lesson of bringing a balance and harmony in daily life.

It was not uncommon for a Sufi *murīd* to perform missionary work and, in this capacity, Daud actually had significant goals to reach. First he had to introduce the ideas of Sufism to audiences who came from all walks of life. He wanted them to realize that there are two equally important aspects to human existence, physical and spiritual. He wished to tell people about the journey a Sufi disciple is required to undertake in order to experience a higher plane of consciousness. He wanted to describe the various experiences a Sufi must undergo to reach spiritual fulfilment. In short, he had to teach the basics of the Sufi philosophy without boring people or scaring them away.

Daud selected the folktale of Cāndā and Lorik to help him accomplish his goals. Needless to say he was not the first to seek to use an interesting story to illustrate a point. However, story telling is an art and we must give Daud credit for telling a popular story with enough skill to keep the interest of his audience.

Why did Lorik leave Govar in the first place with Cāndā after the struggle between Cāndā and his first wife? Mainā already knew about Lorik's affair and if, eventually Lorik had to return to his wife, why make him leave his hometown? Even if the entire story symbolically represents the spiritual journey of a Sufi, what is the specific significance of the homecoming episode?

Once again I repeat what I have said above. When Maulana Daud composed *Cāndāyan* he selected an already popular story only as a point of reference. Daud shaped *Cāndāyan* according to his needs, freely altering its focus.

In *Cāndāyan* the spiritual journey of a Sufi, i.e. Lorik, begins when he sees Cāndā for the first time and swoons. Lorik was invited to a feast at Cāndā's father's house and when he first saw her at her balcony he was convinced that he had seen an *apsara*. The title of this chapter reads: "आमदने चांदा बर कस्र व दीदने लोरिक व बेहोश शुदन लोरिक" (M. Gupta 1967: 150), literally, Cāndā's arrival at the balcony: Lorik's catching a glimpse (of her) and fainting. Lorik fell unconscious and was so disabled that he had to be carried home on a stretcher or *ḍāṇḍ*.

लोरु लीन्ह कइ डान्डी, बिसम्भर कछु न सम्भार। (M. Gupta ed. K. #153)

Some of the people put Lorik on a stretcher;
He became oblivious and beside himself.

The incidents of this episode were perhaps meant to remind the audience of the Biblical story when Moses insisted that he be granted a glimpse of God on Mount Sinai but could not bear to see the Majesty of the Divine face and fainted.[9]

After this incident, Lorik loses all interest in the daily pleasures of life. In his mother Kholin's words:

अब न खाइ अन पानी, दिनहि जाइ कुंबिलात (M. Gupta 1967: 156)

Now he neither eats food nor drinks water.
Day by day he is wasting away.

Lorik now has no recourse but to try to find Cāndā. At this juncture in the story, allegorically, Lorik represents a Sufi novice who has seen a glimpse of the Eternal Beauty and is ready to embark on a mystical journey in her quest.

In line with the tradition of the Prophet, who used to retreat to the solitude of nature, many Sufi orders furnish isolated cells for the practice of the *khalwat*. Discussing the importance of this first step, Laleh Bakhtiar, says that to retreat to an isolated cell in order to 'remember'

God is considered by many Sufis to be the most significant step. Meditation in solitude is an aid in achieving a state of permanent inward retreat (Bakhtiar 1987: 94–5).

In *Cāndāyan*, after seeing Cāndā for the first time, Lorik retreats to a temple, rejects fine clothes, good food and other comforts of life, and stays in seclusion for an entire year practising austerities. During this time he eats only from the forest and uses an animal skin for a blanket:

चितहि चांदा मुख चित उपावइ,
चांद नाम तत सार
एक बरिस लोरिक मढ़ु सेवा (M. Gupta 1967: 164–5)

Holding up the picture of Cāndā in his mind;
Accepting her name as the only essence,
For a year, Lorik participated of the life at the shrine.

The high point of this first stage is to get away from the sophistication of man-made surroundings and retreat to nature to be closer to God. This isolation brings the novice to the threshold of the subsequent stages of his voyage. It provides respite from the worries of daily existence and distances him from his immediate surroundings. Distance provides the seeker with a different perspective.

'If entered into and embraced with sincerity, the stage of the spiritual retreat, that is *khilwat*, has the potential to open the door to the next stage of the mystic journey' (Valiuddin 1977: 152–4).

After practising austerities for a year at the temple, Lorik meets Cāndā again. But his wife Mainā, the symbol of his worldly existence, finds out. The physical fight between Cāndā and Mainā is a symbol for the struggle a person always faces between his spiritual and material pursuits. When a person wishes to disentagle himself from the material comforts of this world to set out in search for his spiritual goals, his path is not easy because difficulties and temptations assail him. Lorik is faced with his mother's mortification, his wife's exasperation, his awkward position in society, and Cāndā's disappointment. In the story, when Lorik pulls Cāndā and Mainā apart after their fist-fight and lets Cāndā escape to her palace, Mainā is quite upset. For her part Cāndā wishes to find out who Lorik is going to be true to.

At this point Lorik is faced with a choice. He takes the next step. He leaves his home and goes across the river with Cāndā. Since in those days and even today, to some extent, most people's wealth is defined by their land and cattle, when Lorik left behind his material possessions, his decision to renounce his wealth spontaneously eased him into the next stage of his journey, i.e. poverty, *faqr. Faqri Fakhri* is a well-known Sufi Motto which means 'I am proud of my state of poverty' (Nicholson 1992: 3).

In Lorik's journey, his ordeal is further intensified during the two snakebite episodes described in detail in the first part of this chapter. It should be noted at this point that the two snakebite episodes leave Lorik a total *faqir*, i.e. completely impoverished.

When a Sufi novice enters seclusion he is trained to engage in constant *zikr*, i.e. the repeated mention of God's attributes. Annemarie Schimmel in her book *The Mystical Dimensions of Islam* writes that in a *khānqāh*, a Sufi master carefully supervised the spiritual development of his disciple. He sends the novice into seclusion and, most importantly, entrusted him with the correct formula for *zikr*. She writes:

> From early days onwards the Sufis dwelt upon the importance of the uninterrupted remembrance of God, *zikr*. They found support in Koranic sentences which invite humankind to remember God often. The regular repetition of certain formulas thousands of times was practised from early days and grew into a central spiritual technique among the brotherhoods. It can be performed aloud or silently. (Schimmel 1975: 111)

In *Cāndāyan*, after she is revived from the first snakebite, Cāndā unfortunately succumbs to a second one. Now Lorik is overcome by grief. He again and again addresses Cāndā and recounts the dangers he had courted to be in her company.

> चांद लागि मइं बहु दुख देखा। गनत न आवइ एक उल्लेखा।।
> बरह मेलि सरगि चढि धाएउं। सिर सेउ खेलि चांद लिएउं आएउं।।

> In Cānda's affection, I experienced such great suffering,
> It is impossible to recount it in one single document.
> Hooking a grappling hook, I climbed up the heavens (terrace);
> Risking my life, I took Cānda and got away with her. (M. Gupta 1967: 321)

In his mystic journey Lorik has so far experienced seclusion, asceticism, poverty, repentance and constant remembrance. Chanting or *zikr*, as discussed before, is believed to bring the Sufi into harmony with the cosmic music. To a mystic, language is a barrier to be annihilated by means of language itself. The body is likened to a reed. The reed-player causes the divine music to flow through his instrument.

Achieving *zikr* helps the disciple to disengage and move away from the self and to concentrate on the Divine. In his efforts to cleanse and purify his soul, the novice expects mercy from God alone. In *Cāndāyan*, lamenting bitterly for Cāndā, Lorik reiterates his staunch faith in God's compassion again and again. He says:

> मोहि न कोइ बिनु दई बिधाता।
> But for you there is none other for me, O my Maker.

Another time Lorik says:

> दुसर न कोउ जो कर उपगारा।
> There is nobody else who will do me a favour.

And then he says,

> सिरजनहार देहि निस्तारा। (M. Gupta 1967: 320)
>
> O Creator, please tide me over.

At this point in time, Lorik has moved from *zikr*, i.e. the stage of constant remembrance on to the stage defined by a Sufi's total faith in God's compassion, i.e. *tawakkul*. To elucidate this next stage of a mystic's journey *tawakkul*, I quote Schimmel again:

> For the first noted ascetic of the East, Ibrahim ibn Adham (d. 777) and his compatriots, one of the most important aspects of true religious life was absolute trust in God, *tawakkul*. For the early Sufis it meant to refrain completely from carrying any money or food when traveling. One trusts in God because there is no bestower of goods but Him. He is the One Who nourishes and has promised that He will care for all the needs of His creatures. (Schimmel 1975: 103)

Moving on to describe the final stage of a mystic's journey, *fanā*, its worth repeating the quotation we looked at earlier:

> The ultimate station, *fanā* is experienced when the seeker loses his self in The Self. His final orientation is towards total receptivity: spiritual death (p. 52). One of the most famous sayings of the Prophet, peace be upon him, is: 'Die before you die.' The tomb room in Konya of Jalal in Din Rumi, the founder of the Mevlevi Order, is actually distinguished as the place of his wedding, for the night of his death is celebrated with all the joy that surrounds a wedding. The *urs* or the wedding of the Sufi saints all over the world is actually their death anniversary celebrated as the day of their annihilation, *fanā*, in the Unity of Being, *wahdat al wajud*. (Bakhtiar 1976: 52)

The concept of getting rid of the body for the sake of releasing the soul or death as salvation is a theme which occurs many times in Maulana Rumi's *Masnavī*. One fine example of this is the *Qissah-i-Tutī* or Tale of the Parrot.[10] It goes as follows.

Once upon a time a Persian merchant had a very accomplished Indian parrot kept in a cage. When came the time for the merchant to go to India again on business, he came to the parrot and asked what it would like the merchant to bring back as a gift. The parrot sent a message with the merchant for the free flocks of parrots in India. In this message he told his free fellow birds of his feelings of suffering and woe in captivity.

When the merchant reached India and chanced upon a flock of parrots which appeared to be similar to his own bird, he delivered his message. On hearing it, a parrot from this flock became afflicted, trembled, and fell. The good merchant was remorseful and cursed himself for having been the bearer of fatal words.

Returning home, he told the entire story to his parrot. As soon as his bird heard about what had happened in India, it also trembled and fell from its perch. Seeing this, the distracted merchant released the listless bird. To his surprise, it flew to a high branch. The merchant asked the parrot to explain this mystery.

The bird told the merchant that it had asked the free birds in India to send back a formula for its release from captivity. The free birds had sent the captive bird a message by example. So long as one serves another, he remains a captive. Only by being indifferent and useless to the external world, does one find freedom. The merchant appreciated this lesson and vowed to follow a new path.

A poet of Urdu has summed up the entire episode in a lovely couplet:

मैंने बुलबुल से जो पूछा दर्दे फुरकत का इलाज
शाख पे तड़पी, तड़प कर गिर पड़ी और मर गई

I asked the nightingale,
What is the medicine for those who suffer in separation?
Upon the perch, turning pale, the nightingale
quivered, collapsed, and died, seized with lamentation.

Schimmel defines this phenomenon as follows:

Fanā is in the first place an ethical concept, i.e., the renunciation of human qualities and increasing spiritualization: it has nothing to do with Indian concept of *nirvana* since it does not mean the attempt to be rescued from the painful cycle of birth and rebirth but rather the return of the creature to the state 'as he was before he was'. (Schimmel 1975: 106)

In the present context, the following famous couplet of the Urdu poet Mirza Asad Allah Khan Ghalib says:

न था कुछ तो खुदा था, कुछ न होता जो खुदा होता।
डुबोया मुझ को होने ने, न होता मैं तो क्या होता।। (Diwan-i-Ghalib #32).

When there was nothing, God was there.
He would still be there, if there was nothing.
It is 'to be' which has done me in.
Guess what would become of me if there were no 'me'?

Following Lorik to the high point of his journey we realize that by the end of the second snakebite episode he has actually arrived at the stage where he can distinguish between true essence and the mirror which merely reflects the Divine Reality. He realizes that he does not wish to survive Cāndā. Without her he feels that his own physical existence is not just painful, it is unbearable. Lorik says:

जरमि न छूट पिरम कर बांधा, पिरम खान्ड आहइ बिस सांधा
जेहि यह चोट लागि सो जानी, कइ लारिक कइ चान्दा रानी

From the handcuffs of love, for the rest of your life, there is no escape,
The dessert of love is certainly laced with poison
Only the wounded understand the pain,
Be it Lorik or be it Lady Cāndā. (M. Gupta 1967: 323)

One of the many poems attributed to Mīrā Bāī opens with,

हे री मैं तो प्रेम दिवानी मेरा दरद ना जाने कोय.

O friend, I am insanely in love, no one knows my pain.

One of the lines of this poem reads:

जौहरी की गति जौहरि जानी, की जिन जौहर होय. (Chaturvedi 1966: 121)

Only one who has already immolated herself
on a funeral pyre can claim to know and understand
what another experiences
when performing the ritual of *Jauhar,* immolating her body on her husband's funeral pyre.

When Cāndā dies after the second snakebite, Lorik decides that he would rather die and accompany her. As Lorik prepared to burn on the funeral pyre, he is prepared to make the ultimate sacrifice, i.e. the sacrifice of his life, his ego, his self. At this moment he is not concerned with his body or with his physical desires (*nafs*). When he is ready to embrace self-annihilation, the ultimate sacrifice, he has actually moved towards union with Eternal Beauty and Joy. In *fanā* he has found life everlasting. In other words, the success of the individual soul in attaining union with the Universal Soul lies in the seriousness of its pursuit and its complete commitment and readiness to sacrifice everything to achieve its goal. Self-sacrifice, then, is the key to *fanā*. In Ibn Farid's words, existence is a veil at the beginning of the mystic life, and during its middle stage, but not at its end. The mystic is veiled at the beginning by the outward view of existence (created things) from the inward view (God), while in the middle state, he is veiled by its inward view from its outward view. But when he has reached his goal, neither do created things veil him from God nor does God veil him from created things, but God reveals Himself to the mystic in both His aspects at once as Creator and as the universe of created things, so that the mystic sees with his bodily eye the beauty of the Divine Essence manifested under the attribute of the Outward.[11]

With reference to the great Persian mystic Bayezid Bistami[12] and his experiences of *fanā*, Annemarie Schimmel writes:

> Bayezid was the first to use the symbolism of the heavenly journey when speaking of his raptures and has described his longing for *fanā* in highly poetical images, as well as his inexplicable disappointment at the end of his experiences. (Schimmel 1975: 106)

In most allegorical stories, the life of a Sufi remains ordinary until the moment of mystic experience imbues it with a quality that makes it quite different from the life of the common man. For example, when the mystic eats, drinks, sleeps and tends to his daily routine he is similar to a common man; but when he is experiencing spiritual ecstasy, it is the high point of his life. Nonetheless, the mystic cannot remain on the high point for long and eventually has to descend to everyday world.

Therefore, after six seasons, or approximately an Indian year, Lorik returns to Govar along with Cāndā. It is by no means an easy task for him to re-enter the life of Govar. He cajoles Mainā into forgiving him for the pain he had caused her. When Lorik and Cāndā arrive home, Lorik's mother Kholin embraces both her daughters-in-law and takes them into the house.

At this point in the story, one may wonder why Lorik could not have accomplished this before the elopement: that would have saved him the dangers, numerous battles and injuries, unbearable sufferings and countless hardships. Perhaps a Sufi's answer would be that Lorik had to experience the *maqāmāt* of *khalvat, faqr, zuhd, zikr, sabr* and *tawakkul* which finally guide him to the stage of *fanā*, so as to infuse his life with meaning. Until having successfully completed his journey he could not return to his family life.

The concept of journey is very important to the Sufis. It reminds the traveller that this world of comfort is just a caravanserai where one stops for but a short time. It forces the traveller to limit the accumulation of worldly possessions and to value spiritual growth. Finally it trains one to look forward to experiencing the unknown. For a Sufi the sound of the camel bells of a caravan is exciting indeed.

Unlike many religious denominations and orders, Islam does not impose celibacy on its clergy. Nonetheless, believers are advised that they should strike a balance between their spiritual and material existence. God says in the Koran that the world along with its beneficial plants, bountiful fruits and animals has been created for the enjoyment of mankind. However, one should beware of extremes and partake of the pleasures of the senses only in moderation.

I would like to reiterate that the most important lesson Daud wished to teach his reader is evident only after the audience has arrived at the last chapter, the homecoming episode. Here Daud demonstrates that balance in life can be achieved by living in harmony with both the spiritual and the physical aspects of life. The full impact of the homecoming episode can be understood only when *Cāndāyan* is viewed in a Sufi context. It is the perfect end to Lorik's story. In fact, it would hardly be an exaggeration to claim that the story could not have culminated in any other way.

NOTES

1. See Jindal 1993: 38.
2. See Schimmel 1994: 12.
3. According to Al-Jili: 'As a mirror in which a person sees the form of himself and cannot see it without the mirror, such is the relation of God to the Perfect Man, who cannot possibly see his own form but in the mirror of the Name Allah; and he is also a mirror to God, for God laid upon Himself the necessity that His Names and attributes should not be seen save in the Perfect Man' (Glasse 1991: 189).
4. In many religious traditions, a tree, because it grows from the earth and reaches to the skies, is a symbolic link between the world of phenomena and the spiritual world. It is often likened to a man who likewise incorporates both physical and spiritual aspects.
5. See Embree 1988: 93.
6. *Fanā* (lit. 'extinction'). In Sufism one hopes 'to die before one dies', that is, to

die to the world and to subsist in God alone; this latter state is called *baqā*, 'subsisting' or, in fact, 'immortality' in the Real (Glasse 1991: 112).

7. Annemarie Schimmel explains the phenomenon of *fanā* as 'debecoming' (Schimmel 1992: 103).
8. For a detailed study of the practice of *Pīrī-murīdī*, see Pinto 1995.
9. The story of Moses comes up in a number of different verses in the Koran. See Glasse 1991: 275.
10. See *The Masnavī* (Nicholson 1977: 85–101).
11. In his *Studies in Islamic Mysticism*, Nicholson dedicates an entire chapter to a discussion of the Odes of Ibn al-Farid (Nicholson 1921: 162–266).
12. Bayazid Bistami was a famous Sufi ascetic from Bistam, near Nishapur. He was associated with the ecstatic rather than with the sober aspect of Sufism. Like Hallaj, he scandalized the orthodox and escaped serious repercussions by pretending to be crazy.

6

Cāndāyan: Indo-Sufi Allegory or *Premākhyān*?

In this concluding chapter, my primary objective is to take up a question that sits at the centre of any critical examination of *Cāndāyan*, namely the question of the genre to which it belongs. This is not a question that pertains to *Cāndāyan* alone. Indeed the same question with equal validity may be asked of *Padmāvat*, *Mṛgāvatī* and other Indian works of similar nature. It is fair to question whether any or all of these works should best be thought of as *masnavīs* or as *premākhyāns*, or something else (e.g. Sufi allegories). Such questions become important to the extent that the nomenclature that we apply affects our reading and understanding of these works. It would be unfortunate if, through the use of an inappropriate rubric under which to characterize these works, we were to miss a significant dimension by means of which it established a linkage with their audience.

In order to facilitate this discussion it is desirable for me to provide further information than I have given so far on a number of representative works composed between the fourteenth and eighteenth centuries. I take *Cāndāyan*, *Padmāvat*, *Mṛgāvatī*, and *Madhumālatī* as representative, of putative *masnavīs* written in India, and *Ḍholā Mārū rā dūhā*, *Mainā-sat*, *Mādhavānal Kāmakandalā*, and *Nala-Damayantī Kathā* as representative of Indian works generally classified as *premākhyāns*. Paralleling the development of 'Sufi' narrative compositions the Hindi *premākhyān* also flourished. The common feature connecting these narratives is the ultimate triumph of love in the face of adversity.[1]

To facilitate a meaningful discussion, only works composed between the fourteenth through the seventeenth centuries will be referred to.[2] *Cāndāyan*, *Padmāvat*, *Mṛgāvatī*, and *Madhumālatī* will be considered as representative compositions of the Indo-Sufi genre and *Ḍholā Mārū rā dūhā, Mainā-sat, Mādhavānal Kāmakandalā* and *Nala-Damayantī Kathā* will represent the *premākhyān*.[3]

It is necessary to be familiar with the above-mentioned works before discussing their characteristics. To this end, brief introductions and plot outlines follow.

Brief Plot Outlines of Representative Indo-Sufi Masnavīs

Mṛgāvatī was composed in 1500 by Kutuban, who lived in Jaunpur.[4] Prince Rājkuwar caught a glimpse of a very unusual female deer, *mṛgī*, on one of his hunting expeditions. Before he could get to it, the deer vanished. The prince became obsessed with the deer. He searched for it for months. One day, the prince arrived by chance at a pond where seven nymphs were bathing. He recognized *Mṛgāvatī* as one of the seven *apsarās*. But before the prince could get closer, the nymphs flew away. The prince found that if he were to steal the very clothes which Mṛgāvatī had left by the side of the pool, she would not be able to get away. So Rājkuwar got a chance to talk with Mṛgāvatī. He convinced her of his love and soon the prince and Mṛgāvatī were united in matrimony.

One day when the prince went away to visit his father, Mṛgāvatī looked for her original clothes and found them. Wearing these, she took off to her father's kingdom in order to test the sincerity of Rājkuwar's devotion. Upon his return, when Rājkuwar learned that Mṛgāvatī had left him, he was deeply distressed. After a number of dangerous expeditions, during one of which he rescued a damsel Rūpmini from a demon, Rājkuwar found Mṛgāvatī. On the way back to his kingdom, he also brought Rūpmini to his palace. Once, when Rājkuwar was hunting, he fell from an elephant and died. His queens committed *satī* at his funeral.

Padmāvat is by far the most famous Indo-Sufi *masnavī*. It was composed by Malik Muhammad Jayasi in 1540.[5] Ratansen, the ruler of Chittor, buys an accomplished parrot who tells him of the incomparable beauty of Padmāvatī, the princess of Siṁhala. Ratansen leaves his kingdom, becomes a yogi, and, after enduring many difficulties, ultimately finds and marries Padmāvatī. In the absence of Ratansen, his wife Nāgamatī suffers the pangs of separation. However, Ratansen returns to Chittor along with Padmāvatī.

Alauddin Khilji learns of Padmāvatī's beauty from a disgruntled Brahmin who had once been associated with Ratansen's court. In the hope of getting Padmāvatī, Alauddin decides to attack Chittor. In the meanwhile, however, Ratansen is killed in another battle. Both Nāgamatī and Padmāvatī immolate themselves on their husband's funeral pyre. Ultimately, Chittor falls to Alauddin, but Padmāvatī does not.[6]

Madhumālatī was composed by Manjhan in 1545.[7] Prince Manohar was taken, while asleep, by some nymphs to Princess Madhumālatī, to see if the two would make a suitable couple. Leaving them asleep side by side, the nymphs went off. When Manohar and Madhumālatī awoke, they fell in love. Having returned, the nymphs were remorseful at what had happened and took Manohar back to his palace. The prince burned with the fire of separation. He become a jogi and set out in search of Madhumālatī. After having faced many dreadful and seemingly hopeless situations, he finally found Madhumālatī. They were married and she came to live with him in his palace.

Brief Plot Outline of the Non-Sufi Premākhyāns

Ḍholā Mārū rā dūhā, a love story, is widely considered to be the oldest of the non-Sufi *premākhyāns*.[8] For a long time, this folktale existed in an oral form in the couplet meter *dūhā/dohā*. The poet's name is still uncertain. It can be accompanied by music. No critical edition of this composition has been published so far. Three recorded versions are available. Kushal Lābh's version was recomposed in 1560.[9] In the course of the text, Kushal Lābh says that he has composed his *Ḍholā Mārū rā dūhā*[10] in the *caupāī* meter out of *dūhās* which were already in existence.[11] The following story sums up Kushal Lābh's *Ḍholā Mārū rā dūhā*.

Prince Ḍholā and Princess Māravaṇī were married to each other as children under unusual circumstances. Both continued to live with their respective parents. When Ḍholā became a young man, he married another princess. When Māravaṇī became a young woman, she saw her husband Ḍholā in a dream. Now she wished to be with her husband. Many messages were sent to invite Ḍholā to come and get his bride, but to no avail. However, when Māravaṇī sent a message describing to Ḍholā her longing and suffering in his absence, he too experienced feelings of love for Māravaṇī. He set out to bring her home. After the *gaunā*[12] ceremony and associated festivities Ḍholā brought his bride back to his palace.

Mainā-sat was composed by Sadhan around 1567.[13] Like *Cāndāyan*, it was inspired by the folktale of Loriki. Mainā was a chaste woman. Her husband had eloped with another woman. In her husband's absence, the local prince, who wants Mainā's favours, sends a woman, Ratnā, to plead with her. Ratnā tries to convince Mainā that she should forsake her loyalty and devotion to Lorik because he was not true to her. Mainā, however, in a *bārahmāsā*, describes her own suffering and repeats her vow of loyalty to her husband Lorik to her last breath. As Mainā was pledging herself, once again, to Lorik, she realized that Ratnā was nothing but a pimping bawd and had her head shaved. Ratnā was paraded through the city streets.

Mādhavānal Kāmakandalā is the love story of the courtesan Kāmakandalā and the Brahmin Mādhavānal, inspired by a Sanskrit composition of the same name. *Mādhavānal Kāmakandalā* is also known as *Mādhavānala-Ākhyānaṁ* or *Mādhavānala Nāṭakaṁ*. It was composed by Ānandadhar in approximately 1300.[14] Since then, this work has inspired many non-Sufi as well as Sufi narrative compositions.[15]

In most recensions, the plot develops along the following lines. Mādhava and Kāmakandalā are incarnations of Kāmadeva and Rati, the god and goddess of beauty and love. Mādhava, the handsome and accomplished brahmin, is a courtier of King Govinda Candra of Puṣpāvatī city. The young women of Puṣpāvatī are all in love with Mādhava, so the king banishes him from Puṣpāvatī. Mādhava finds a position at king Kāmasena's court and falls in love with the royal courtesan Kāmakandalā. When Kāmasena learns of this he too orders Mādhava to leave town. In great distress, Mādhava seeks help from Vikramāditya in Ujjayani. After testing Mādhava, Vikramāditya is convinced of his love for Kāmakandalā. He declares war on Kāmasena. Kāmakandalā also undergoes tests to prove that her devotion for Mādhava is steadfast. Finally, the two lovers are reunited by Vikramāditya.[16] They marry.

Nala-Damayantī Kathā was inspired by the story of Rājā Nala and his wife Damayantī in the *Mahābhārata* (the *Nalopākhyāna* of the *Vanaparva*).[17] Later poems such as Śrīharṣa's *Naiṣadhīya-caritam*, composed in Sanskrit,[18] and Faizi's *Nal-Daman*, in Persian,[19] were also inspired by the *Nalopākhyāna*.

Narapati Vyas of Ujjain composed his *Nala-Damayantī Kathā* around 1575. Except for a few new episodes, the storyline follows that in the *Mahābhārata*.[20] Rājā Nala heard of the beauty of Damayantī and went to her *svayaṁvara*.[21] At the same time, Damayantī fell in love with Nala and selected him as her husband. Later, Nala gambled away his entire kingdom to his brother. He had to go live in the forest with Damayantī. One day, Nala abandoned Damayantī as she slept. Upon waking up in the woods, not finding Nala, Damayantī was terrified. Hearing her cries, a hunter approached her and made advances which were repulsed. Damayantī experienced terrible hardships and sufferings as she searched for Nala. Nala, who was very knowledgeable in appraising horses, lived in disguise and took up a job as a chariot driver. Ultimately the two lovers were reunited at a 'second *svayaṁvara*'.[22]

Distinctive Features of the Indo-Sufi Masnavī *and the* Premākhyān *Tradition*

The Indo-Sufi narratives and the *premākhyān* traditions share many common features. Both turn to a common pool of literature and folktales for material. Within the body of the text, a picture, a dream, or a description of the beloved acts as the agent which plants the seeds of love; the guru or the spiritual preceptor plays a significant role; the hero and the heroine often have a friend to help them through crucial situations. The friend often acts as a messenger.

We shall now discuss those features which contribute to the construction of the respective identities of the Indo-Sufi narratives and the *premākhyān* traditions.

In the *premākhyān* tradition, the narrative focuses on the chastity of the heroine. Her singular devotion to her husband is tested again and again, with regard to her physical purity and self-restraint in the face of temptation. Her suffering exceeds that of the hero by far. In *Ḍholā Mārū rā dūhā*, Ḍholā is unmindful of his betrothal to Mārvaṇī and marries another. In *Mainā-sat*, Lorik runs away with another woman, leaving his wife unprotected. In all four of the *premākhyāns* in question, the heroine suffers unspeakable hardships in the absence of her husband. In *Mainā-sat, Mādhavānal Kāmakandalā*, and *Nala-Damayantī Kathā* the heroines are tempted to have physical relations with men other than their husbands. This situation, when a woman is tested for fidelity and loyalty to her husband, is called *satītva parīkṣā*, the test of chastity.[23] The physical chastity of the heroine is a powerful symbol of emotional and spiritual commitment and can be equated with spiritual power. Eventually, the heroine of the *premākhyān* tradition is reunited with her husband.

Such values are not observed in the Indo-Sufi *masnavī* tradition, where it is the suffering and commitment of the hero that draws our attention. The sincerity of the hero is submitted to numerous difficult tests. Compared with the sufferings of Cāndā, Padmāvatī, Mṛgāvatī and

Madhumālatī, the difficulties that Lorik endures and the risks he takes in order to be with Cāndā, the perils through which Ratansen passes to meet Padmāvatī, the pain which Rājkuwar bears in Mṛgāvatī's absence and the trials Manohar endures to get to Madhumālatī, are far more trying and of longer duration. In the *masnavī*, the description of the hero's suffering in separation, *viraha*, plays the same role as the description of the heroine's *satītva* in the *premākhyān*.

In the *masnavī* the heroine is often uncompassionate, at times deliberately inconsiderate with regard to the condition of the suffering hero. The hero has to prove his sincerity and commitment by going through extended ordeals. In *Cāndāyan*, when Lorik tries to climb the palace balcony by throwing a scaling hook, Cāndā deliberately and repeatedly disengages the device. Similarly, in *Padmāvat*, even when Ratansen gives up everything and finally arrives in Siṁhala, Padmāvatī finds him immature. In *Mṛgāvatī*, also, the heroine abandons the hero to test his devotion.

On the other hand, the hero of the *premākhyān* often demonstrates indifference to the heroine's suffering. In *Ḍholā Mārū rā dūhā*, many messages are sent to Ḍholā to come and get Mārū, but he does not respond. Similarly, Lorik and Raja Nala leave their wives in impossible situations.

In the representative *premākhyāns* selected for this study, with the exception of *Mādhavānal Kāmakandalā*, the heroine is married to the hero. At the end of *Mādhavānal Kāmakandalā*, Mādhava and Kāmakandalā, too, get married. In the *masnavī*, however, it is not necessary for the hero and heroine to be man and wife. Lorik and Ratansen are married men when they fall in love with Cāndā and Padmāvatī respectively. Early in *Cāndāyan*, Cāndā is married off to Bawan but does not show unconditional commitment to him. Usually the heroine of the *masnavī* is already married to another at the outset. Thus, in contrast to the *premākhyān* tradition, the heroine's body is not a symbol of her spirit.

Muslims do not believe in reincarnation. Therefore, unlike *premākhyān* narratives, *masnavīs* make few references to incidents in a previous birth.

Most *premākhyāns* have a happy ending. Love triumphs over adverse circumstances, misfortune having been averted due to the colossal strength of the heroine's character and her spiritual power. The heroine is reunited with her husband and they live happily ever after. When

Ḍholā comes to fetch Māravaṇī it spells the end of her misfortunes and sufferings. The *Mādhavānal Kāmakandalā premākhyān* ends in the marriage of Mādhava and Kāmakandalā.

This feature is not consistently found in *masnavī* narratives. The story never ends when the hero and the heroine are finally united. In fact, it goes on to show the hero living with both his wife and his beloved. Sometimes the story ends with the death of the hero. In some Sufi narratives, when the hero is killed, his wife and/or beloved immolate themselves on his funeral pyre. In *Padmāvat*, Ratansen is killed in battle and Padmāvatī and Nāgamatī commit *satī*. Similarly, Rājkuwar, the hero of *Mṛgāvatī*, dies in a hunting accident and his wives throw themselves on his funeral pyre.

The most significant difference between the *premākhyān* and the Sufi narratives, however, is that a *masnavī* is an allegorical romance. This simply means that the story can be interpreted at two different levels, secular and spiritual. On the secular level, the *masnavī* is not all that different from the *premākhyān*, in the sense that both serve similar purposes, providing entertainment, pleasure, information and lessons to the audience. Most *premākhyāns*, however, resist allegorical interpretation.

On the spiritual level, as discussed above, the hero of the *masnavī* represents the human soul. According to the Koran, the soul is sent to the phenomenal world charged with certain duties and goals. These duties are known as the pillars of Islam. They include *namāz, ruzā* (fasting), and *zakāt* (charity). Such duties keep a person in constant touch with his own spirituality. The premise behind them is that the soul must remain mindful of its relationship to God during its stay on Earth. However, in this world of colour and aroma, *duniya-i-rang-o-bū*, the individual gets lost in the enjoyment of secular life. The wife of the hero in the Indo-Sufi *masnavī* often represents his worldly life. At a certain moment, he gets a glimpse of the heroine, the symbol of the Eternal Beloved. The hero must find his beloved, but does not know how. He needs a teacher to guide him. Only a teacher who has already attained the 'state of knowing' can show him the appropriate path. Only by giving up the luxuries of this world, by practising austerities in the forest, and by facing difficulties does the hero ultimately fulfil his spiritual goals. His sufferings are likened to the spiritual stations a Sufi seeker must experience before he can attain his ultimate destination.

In the *masnavī* tradition, the physical beauty of the heroine is merely an instrument leading the hero to Eternal Beauty. It is not an end in itself. The lover sees God's beauty in the heroine. Thus the *nakha-śikha varṇan* of the beloved's beauty has a purpose.[24] According to Rizvi:

> The *nakh-shikh* of the *Chanda'in* made a deep impact on later writers of Hindi *masnawis* and were reproduced chiefly because of the great prestige of its author as a mystic. Cāndā's beauty is described allegorically as a piece of unreachable fruit. The Persian translation of *Chanda'in* indicates the extent to which the text could be reconciled with Persian ideas of mysticism. The analogy is subtle: Mystics get a glimpse of the Supreme but God Himself is beyond their reach. (Rizvi 1986: 365–6)

Because the heroine represents Universal Soul, the *masnavīs* describe the splendour of her cities, palace, and apartments.[25]

Scholars of Hindi literature have classified the bulk of Indo-Sufi narratives in different ways. For example, Ramchandra Shukla calls this genre *premagāthā*[26] or love stories; Sharan and Rastogi call it *laukika sāhitya*[27] or worldly literature; Tripathi calls it *madhya kālīna sāhitya*[28] or medieval literature; and P. Gupta calls it '*premākhyān*'[29] or love narratives.

Nevertheless, modern scholars have suggested that Indo-Sufi literature cannot be discussed under the general category of 'medieval Hindi literature', *premākhyān*, or *premgāthā*. Among scholars advocating a distinct and separate identity for the *masnavī* are Dwivedi, Pandey, Batra, and Yash Gulati. Arguing for the need to recognize Sufi poetry as a distinct genre, Yash Gulati says that, traditionally, historians of Hindi literature have divided literature composed in the *bhakti kāl* into two sub-categories, *saguṇa* (with attributes) and *nirguṇa* (without attributes) *bhakti kāvya*. In this way, directly or indirectly, the very existence of the Indo-Sufi literary genre has been denied. According to Gulati, Ganapati Chandra Gupta was the first scholar who, 'in a scientific manner', tried to argue that the existence of a separate and distinctive Indo-Sufi *masnavī* genre is a fallacy (Gulati 1979: 11).

Gulati chuckles at the arguments some scholars have presented in order to deny the Indo-Sufi *masnavī* a distinct identity. He considers these excuses to be absurd. In the course of these arguments it is alleged that the authors were often Hindu and therefore, not compelled to familiarize people with Sufi beliefs; that the aim of the Muslim poets was to acquire fame and to entertain, not to propagate religion; that in this literature it is Indian rather than Sufi philosophy that finds expression; that there is no spiritualism in these so-called 'Sufi' love stories; that many of these work can be interpreted in terms of Indian philosophy;[30] that most of the stories draw inspiration from Indian sources and show respect for Hindu deities; and that the style of love expressed in them is Indian. The language, prosody, and style bear evidence that these narratives are nothing but Hindi *premgāthās* (Gulati 1979: 13).

Gulati goes on to say that although it is true that a large number of the poets who composed Hindi love narratives in the medieval period were Hindu, it is highly improbable that all of them shared the same goals and objectives. The hero of *Ḍholā mārū* does not see divine beauty reflected in his beloved. In *Mainā-sat*, Lorik is a different character than the hero of Daud's *Cāndāyan*. In *Padmāvat*, according to Dviwedi, Jayasi never let go of a single opportunity to point out the hidden meaning of what is obvious and transparent. He always sings the praises of the Unseen. Similarly, Chandrabali Pandey says that the *kaḍvaks* of the Indo-Sufi *masnavīs* are packed with spirituality (Gulati 1979: 17–18). Therefore, the fact that the 'Sufi' narratives are essentially allegorical romances lends them a distinctive identity.

It could be argued that because in many Indo-Sufi *masnavīs*, the fact that the hero and the heroine meet at a temple, that the hero often becomes a jogi and is described in terms of those who follow the Nāth and Siddha paths, and features such as the constant respectful mention of Hindu gods and goddesses, description of Hindu festivals and holy places, adoption of Indic prosody, and borrowing from the Indic literary and folk materials, all may have contributed to the confusion that Indo-Sufi literature is essentially the same as the Hindi *premākhyān*.

Asani and others have pointed out the need for a re-examination of literature classified under the rubric of the Indic *masnavī*. I agree with him in that the term '*masnavi*' is too broad and does not explicitly address significant issues.

Thus the term gives the reader no clue as to whether *masnavīs* composed in India in Persian language and meter (such as the *masnavīs* of Amir Khusrau) are included. Should poetic works based on local folk romances composed in vernacular languages such as Punjabi, Bengali, and Sindhi and interpreted in mystic terms, for example, *Hīr-Rānjhā* and *Sassi-Punnuh*, be counted as Indo-Sufi *masnavīs*? If so, how can the sharp differences in prosody and rhyme be reconciled?[31]

If the rubric is changed from 'Indo-Sufi *masnavī*' to 'Hindi Sufi *masnavī*' to separate narratives composed in Awadhī from those composed in Bengali, Sindhi, and Punjabi, then should the Bengali, Sindhi, and Punjabi compositions be kept under the *premākhyān* classification, or should they be studied as a single category of non-Hindi Indo-Sufi *masnavī* compositions? Alternatively, should different criteria be used with regard to the *masnavī* of various individual languages?

As for the question of the identity of the 'Sufi' narratives composed in Awadhī, I agree with Asani and Gulati's argument. I have attempted to explain in detail that the Indo-Sufi *masnavī* literature differs significantly from the Hindi *premākhyān* genre. The Indo-Sufi *masnavī* deserves a separate classification, re-examination, and re-evaluation within medieval Hindi literature. It is not to be classified as a subcategory of the *madhya yugīn premākhyān* genre. And this is not a mere terminological quibble. It is crucial to any understanding of the nature of this genre in its historical and cultural context.

Should *Cāndāyan*, then, be considered only as a *masnavī*, or is it a *premākhyān* as well? In my opinion the story of the *premākhyān Mainā-sat* is an indispensable and integral part of the *Cāndāyan* narrative. The description of the suffering of Lorik pining for Cāndā is as significant as the description of the suffering of Mainā pining for Lorik. In fact, in *Cāndāyan*, the role of Lorik can be compared to a fulcrum which balances a pair of scales. As indicated in Chapter 5, Mainā symbolizes Lorik's worldly life and Cāndā represents the spiritual aspect of his individual being. Therefore Lorik's quest for Cāndā and his return home to Mainā are inseparable and equally significant features of *Cāndāyan*. Thus I am justified in claiming that *Cāndāyan* enjoys a unique position in the Hindi literature of the medieval period. *Cāndāyan* is both an instance of the Indo-Sufi *masnavī* as well as a *premākhyān*.

NOTES

1. See Pandey 1982: 83.
2. See Sharan and Rastogi 1988: 87.
3. See S.M. Pandey's discussion on the topic of the non-Sufi love narratives composed in the fourteenth to seventeenth centuries, in *Sūfī premākhyān sāhitya* (Pandey 1982: 121–55).
4. See M. Gupta 1968: 3.
5. See Jindal 1993: 40–3 for details.
6. See M. Gupta 1963.
7. See Table 1.1.
8. Shyam Manohar Pandey writes: '*Dholā Mārū rā dūhā* is considered to be the first available non-Sufi composition in the Hindi *premākhyān* tradition. It could have been composed in its oral form in approximately 1000. However none of

its recorded versions dates from before the fourteenth century' (S.M. Pandey 1982: 122).

9. See *Ḍholā Mārū rā dūhā*, 1935, Kashi: Nagari Pracharini Sabha.
10. See S.M. Pandey 1982: 123.
11. For a discussion of the *dohā* and the *caupāī* meters, see Chapter 3.
12. When child-marriage was customary, the bride and the groom stayed with their respective parents until puberty. When the marriage was consummated, the ceremony was called *gaunā*.
13. See S.M. Pandey 1982: 135.
14. See Keith 1928: 293.
15. See S.M. Pandey 1982: 138.
16. The reader may find features similar to this in the Biblical story of Joseph.
17. *Mahābhārata* (Buck 1973: 119–38).
18. See Keith 1928: 139.
19. See Beale 1971: 125.
20. For a detailed description of the new episodes in this work, see S.M. Pandey 1982: 136.
21. *Svayaṁ* means 'self', *vara* means 'choice'. The Sanskrit word *svayaṁvara* refers to a custom which gave the bride an opportunity to select her own husband.
22. Actually there was no second *svayaṁvara*. For a complete explanation, see Buck 1973: 135–6.
23. *Satītva parīkṣā* episodes in the *premākhyān* narratives are powerful reminders of Sītā's abduction by Rāvaṇa, his efforts to win over her love, and her humiliating test by fire, in the *Rāmāyaṇa*. See O'Flaherty 1975: 201–2.

    The story of princess Sāvitrī whose devotion brought her husband Satyavān back to life is also relevant. See Walker 1983: 362.
24. For a detailed discussion of Sufi symbols in the Indo-Sufi *masnavī* literature see the following:

    Bhala Chandra Tiwari's *Sūfī Kāvya meṁ Nārī*;

    '*Cāndāyan* meṁ nakha-śikha aur uskā ādhyātmika rūpa' in S.M. Pandey's *Sufi Kāvya Vimarśa*, pp. 1–26;

    'Premākhyānoṁ kī pratīka yojanā' in S.M. Pandey's *Madhya Yugīna Premākhyāna*, pp. 261–84;

    Sarojini Pandey's *Hindi Sūfī Kāvya meṁ Pratīka Yojanā*;

    Vidhyadhar Tripathi's *Jayasī ke Sāhitya meṁ Aprastuta Yojanā: Jāyasī sāhitya meṁ prayukta upmānoṁ kī sūcī*;

    Shivasahay Pathak's *Hindi Sūfī Kāvya kā Samagra Anuśīlana*;

    Parashuram Chaturvedi's *Sūfī Kāvya Saṁgraha*, pp. 84–95;

    Shrinivas Batra's *Hindi aur Fārasī Sūfī Kāvya kā Tulanātmaka Adhyayana*, pp. 209–312; and

    Sudha Saksena's *Jāyasī kī Bimba Yojanā*.
25. This description may be an extension of the description of the heavens in the Koran.

26. See *Hindi sāhitya kā itihās* (Sabha 1965: 101).
27. See *Hindi sāhitya kā itihās* (Mandir 1988: 139).
28. See Vidhyadhar Tripathi's *Jāyasī ke Sāhitya meṁ Aprastuta Yojanā: Jāyasī sāhitya meṁ prayukta upmanoṁ kī sūcī* (1978: 7).
29. P. Gupta (1964: 20).
30. Towards the end of his *masnavī Padmāvat*, Jayasi provides a key to the symbols he uses in his text. For example, he stipulates that Raja Ratansen is a symbol of the human soul. Padmāvatī is a symbol of Eternal Beauty, and the kingdom of Chittor is the corporeal body. There is a pun on the word 'Chittor'. It can be broken into two words, '*cita*' and '*ura*', respectively meaning 'heart' and 'mind'.
31. See Schimmel's *History of Classical Literatures*.

Bibliography

Adilshah II, Ebrahim, *Kitāb-i-Nauras*, New Delhi: Caxton, 1956.

Ahmad, Akbar, *Discovering Islam*, New Delhi: Vistaar, 1990.

Ahmad, Manazir, *Sultan Firoz Shah Tughlaq*, Allahabad: Chugh, 1977.

Ahmad, Nazir, ed., *Kitāb-i-Nauras*, New Delhi: Bharatiya Kala Kendra, 1956.

———, 'The Influence of Persian and Persian Culture in India', *Indo-Iranica*, 1985, p. 37.

Ali, Yusuf, trans., *The Holy Quran*, Lahore: Shaikh Muhammad Ashraf, 1934.

Ameer, A.A., *Amīr Alī Amīr kī Ghazaleṁ*, Raipur: Haji Mohsin Ali Sohail, 1995.

Apte, V.S., *Sanskrit-English Dictionary*, 1890, Delhi: Motilal Banarsidass, rpt., 1976.

Arberry, A.J., *Sufism: An Account of the Mystics of Islam*, London: Allen & Unwin, 1950.

———, *Classical Persian Literature*, London: Allen & Unwin, 1958.

———, *Tales from the Masnavī*, London: George Allen & Unwin, 1961.

———, *More Tales from the Masnavī*, London: George Allen & Unwin, 1963.

———, *An Introduction to the History of Sufism*, New Delhi: Rekha, 1992.

Arnold, T.W., *Painting in Islam*, New York: Dover, 1965.

Aryanpur, Abbas, and Manochehr, *The Combined New Persian-English and English-Persian Dictionary*, Lexington: Mazda, 1986.

Asani, A.S., *The Būjh Niranjan: An Ismāīlī Mystical Poem*, Cambridge: Harvard Center for Middle Eastern Studies, 1991.

———, 'The Bridegroom in the Medieval Sindhi Poetry', in *Studies in South Asian Devotional Literature*, ed. A. Entwistle and F. Mallison, New Delhi: Manohar, 1991.

——— and Kamal Abdel-Malek in collaboration with Annemarie Schimmel, *Images of the Prophet in Popular Muslim Poetry*, Columbia: University of South Carolina Press, 1995.

Asvaghosa, *Saundarānanda*, ed. Rama Shankar Tripathi, Varanasi: Krsnadasa Akademi, 1992.

Atish, A.S., *Tarh-i-Ārūz-i-Pārasī*, Tehran: Sazman Intsharat Faruhar, 1987.

Attar, F., *The Conference of the Birds*, trans. Afkham Darbandi and Dick L. Davis, Harmondsworth: Penguin, 1984.

Bahari, Hardev, *Persian Influence on Hindi*, Allahabad: Bharati Press, 1960.

Bakhtiar, Laleh, *Sufi Expressions of the Mystic Quest*, New York: Thames and Hudson, 1987.

Baldick, Julian, *Mystical Islam: An Introduction to Sufism*, New York: New York University Press, 1989.

Barani, Zia ud-Din, *Tarikh-i-Firoz Shahi*, trans. H.M. Elliot, ed. John Dowson, Lahore: Jasarat, 1974.

Basham, A.L., *The Wonder that was India*, New York: Grove, 1959.

Batra, Srinivas, *Hindī aur Fārasī Sūfī Kāvya kā Tulanātmak Adhyayan*, Varanasi: Nagari Sabha, 1973.

Bayat, Mojdeh, and M.A. Jamnia, *Tales from the Land of the Sufis*, Boston: Shambhala, 1994.

Beale, T.W., *An Oriental Biographical Dictionary*, New Delhi: Manohar, rpt., 1971.

Beeston, A.F.L., T.M. Johnstone, R.B. Serjeant, and G.R. Smith, eds., *Arabic Literature to the End of the Umayyad Period*, Melbourne: Cambridge University Press, 1983.

Behari, Bankey, *Mystics and Yogis of India*, Bombay: Bharatiya Vidya Bhavan, 1962.

Bhayani, H.C., *Apabhraṁśa Language and Literature: A Short Introduction*, Delhi: B.L. Institute of Indology, 1987.

Blackburn, Stuart H., Peter J. Claus, Joyce B. Fluckiger, and Susan S. Wadley, eds., *Oral Epics in India*, Berkeley: University of California Press, 1989.

Blochmann, H., ed., *Ain-i-Akbari*, Lahore: Qasain Reprint, 1975.

———, *Majmual*, Bahrain: Bibliotheca Indica, 1983.

Brown, Charles Philip, *Sanskrit Prosody and Numerical Symbols*, New Delhi: Asian Publication Services, 1981.

Browne, Edward G., *A Literary History of Persia*, vol. 1, New York: Charles Scribner's Sons, 1902.

———, *A Literary History of Persia*, vol. 2, Cambridge: Cambridge University Press, 1928.

Bryant, K., *Poems to the Child God*, Berkeley: University of California Press, 1978.

———, 'Three-three-two versus four-by-four: metrical frames for the padas of Surdas', in *Devotional Literature in South Asia: Current Research, 1985–1988*, ed. R.S. McGregor, Cambridge: Cambridge University Press, 1992.

Buck, William, trans., *Mahabharata*, Berkeley: University of California Press, 1973.

Chandra Sansar, *Some Prominent Muslim-Hindi Poets*, Delhi: Atmaram, 1986.

Chatterji, Suniti Kumar, *Iranianism*, Calcutta: The Asiatic Society, 1972.

Chatterji, Sukumar Sen, *A Middle Indo-Aryan Reader*, Calcutta: Calcutta University, 1960.

Chaturvedi, P., *Sūfī Kāvya Saṁgrah*, Prayag: Hindi Sahitya Sammelan, 1965.

———, *Mīrābāī kī Padāwalī*, Prayag: Hindi Sahitya Sammelan, 1966.

Chittick, W.C., *The Sufi Path of Love: The Spiritual Teachings of Rumi*, Albany: State University of New York Press, 1983.

———, *The Sufi Path of Knowledge*, Albany: State University of New York Press, 1989.

Classe, Cyril, *The Concise Encyclopedia of Islam*, San Francisco: Harper Collins, 1991.

Cobham, Catherine, *A Introduction to Arab Poetics*, Austin: University of Texas Press, 1990.

Cowan, J.M., ed., *The Hans Wehr Dictionary of Modern Written Arabic*, New York: Spoken Language Services, Inc., 1976.

Damodara, Motichand, *Ukti-Vyakti-Prakaraṇa: Parallel Illustrations in Old Kosali of the 12th century*, ed. Jina Vijaya Muni, Linguistic Study of Old Kosali by S.K. Chatterji, Bombay: Bharatiya Vidya Bhavan, 1953.

Dastagardi, Vahid, ed. and trans., *Kulliyat-i-Nizami Ganjavi (1372)*, 2 vols, Tehran: Intisharat-i-Nigah, 1993.

Dawood, N.J., trans., *Koran*, Harmondsworth: Penguin, 1974.

Deva, B. Chaitanya, *Musical Instruments of India: Their History and Development*, 2nd rev. edn., New Delhi: Munshiram Manoharlal, 1987.

Dhar, Lakshmi, ed., *Padumavati: A Linguistic Study of the 16th Century Hindi (Awadhi) by Lakshmidhar*, London: Luzac, 1949.

Dowson, John, ed., *Tarikh-i-Firoz Shahi*, Lahore: Jasarat Printers, 1974.

Dwivedi, Hazariprasad, *Hindi Sāhitya kī Bhūmika*, Bombay: Hindi Granth Ratnakar, 1963.

———, *Hindi Sāhitya*, Delhi: Attarchand Kapur and Sons, 1964.

Dwivedi, Ram Awadh, *A Critical Survey of Hindi Literature*, Delhi: Motilal Banarsidass, 1966.

Eaton, H.F., *Sufis of Bijapur*, Princeton: Princeton University Press, 1978.

Eck, Diana L. and Françoise Mallison, eds., *Devotion Divine: Bhakti Traditions from the Regions of India*, Paris: Ecole Française d'Extreme-Orient, 1991.

Embree, Ainslie T., ed., *Sources of Indian Tradition*, 2 vols., New York: Columbia University Press, 1988.

Endress, G., *An Introduction to Islam*, trans. C. Hillenbrand, New York: Columbia University Press, 1988.

Entwistle, Alan E., *Braj: Centre of Krishna Pilgrimage*, Groningen: Egbert Forsten, 1987.

Entwistle, Alan E., 'Indian Prosody', in *The New Princeton Encyclopedia of Poetry and Poetics*, ed. Alex Preminger, T.V.F. Brogan, Frank J. Warnke, O.B. Hardison, Jr., and Earl Miner, Princeton: Princeton University Press, 1993 (p. 603). The article cites the article of V. Raghavan, 'Sanskrit and Prakrit Metres', *Journal of the Madras University* 23 (1952–3).

——— and Françoise Mallison, eds., *Studies in South Asian Devotional Literature*, New Delhi: Manohar, 1991.

Ernst, C.W., *Eternal Garden: Mysticism, History and Politics at a South Asian Sufi Center*, Albany: State University of New York Press, 1992.

Falconer, A.E.I., *Sufi Literature and the Journey to Immortality*, Delhi: Motilal Banarsidass, 1991.

Fitzgerald, E., ed. and trans., *Rubaiyat Khayyam*, 1868, Tehran: Bank Melli Iran Press, rpt., 1964.

Gaeffke, Peter, 'Alexander and the Bengali Sufis', in *Studies in South Asian Devotional Literature*, ed. A. Entwistle and F. Mallison, New Delhi: Manohar, 1994.

Gelder, Van G.J.H., *Beyond the Line: Studies in Arabic Literature*, Leiden: E.J. Brill, 1982.

Gelpke, Rudolf, ed. and trans., *The Story of Layla and Majnun of Nizami*, Oxford: Cassimer, 1966.

Ghalib, Asadullah Khan, *Dīvan-i-Ghālib*, ed. Malikram, Delhi: Ghalib Institute Publications, 1979.

Ghulam Mustafa, Hafiz, *Religious Trends in Pre-Islamic Arabic Poetry*, Aligarh: Aligarh Muslim University Press, 1971.

Glasse, Cyril, *The Concise Encyclopedia of Islam*, San Francisco: Harper, 1989.

Growse, F.S., ed., *The Ramayana*, Delhi: Motilal Banarsidass, 1987.

Grunebaum, G.E. von, ed., *Arabic Poetry: Theory and Development*. Wiesbaden: Otto Harrassowitz, 1973.

Guillaume, A., *Islam*, Edinburgh: Penguin, 1954.

Gulati, Yash, *Sūfī Kavitā kī Pahcān*, New Delhi: Pravin Prakashan, 1979.

Gupta, Mataprasad, ed., *Manjhana kṛta Madhumālatī: Bhūmikā, Sampādita pāṭha, Pāṭhāntara, Artha aura Śabdānukramaṇī*, Allahabad: Mitra Prakashan, 1961.

———, ed., *Padmāvata*, Allahabad: Bharati Bhandar Leader Press, 1963(a).

———, ed., *Raula Vela aur uskī bhāsā*, Prayag: Mitra Prakashan, 1963(b).

———, *Madhumālatī Vārtā*, Varanasi: Nagari Sabha, 1964.

———, ed., *Cāndāyan*, Agra: Durga Printing Works, 1967.

———, ed., *Mṛgāvatī*, Agra: Durga Printing Works, 1968.

Gupta, M.G., *Indian Mysticism: Rigveda to Radhasoami Faith*, Agra: M.G. Publishers, 1993.

———, *Mystic Symbolism in Ramayan, Mahabharat, and the Pilgrim's Progress*, Agra: M.G. Publishers, 1993.

Gupta, Parameshwarilal, ed., *Cāndāyan*, Bombay: Hindi Granth Ratnakar, 1964.

Haeri, F.S., *The Journey of the Self*, San Francisco: Harper Collins, 1991.

Halbfass, Wilhelm, *India and Europe: An Essay in Understanding*, Albany: State University of New York Press, 1988.

Hamori, Andras, *On the Art of Medieval Arabic Literature*, Princeton: Princeton University Press, 1974.

Handa, R.L., *History of Hindi Language and Literature*, Bombay: Bharatiya Vidya Bhavan, 1978.

Hardy, P., *Historians of Medieval India: Studies in Indo-Muslim Historical Writing*, London: Luzac, 1960.

Hawley, J.S., *Sur Das: Poet, Singer, Saint*, Seattle: University of Washington Press, 1984.

Hillenbrand, Carole, ed., *An Introduction to Islam*, New York: Columbia University Press, 1988.

Holt, P.M., Ann K.S. Lambton and Bernard Lewis, eds., *The Cambridge History of Islam*, Cambridge: Cambridge University Press, 1970.

Idris, Shah, *The Sufis*, New York: Anchor Books/Doubleday, 1971.

Ikram, S.M., *Muslim Civilization in India*, New York: Columbia University Press, 1964.

Irwin, Robert, 'Mystical Islam: An Introduction to Sufism', Reviewed by Julian Baldick, in *Religion* (4 December 1989).

Jackson, A.W., *Early Persian Poetry, from the Beginnings to Firdausi*, New York: Macmillan, 1920.

Jain, Hiralal, ed., *Ṇāyakumāracariu*, Banares: Bharatiya Jnanapitha Prakashan, 1944.

Jalal al-Din Rumi, Maulana, *Mathnavi of Jalalu'ddin Rumi*, trans. and commentary R.A. Nicholson, Cambridge: University Printing House, 1977.

Jauhari, R.C., *Firoz Tughluq*, Jalandhar: Cosmic Printers, 1990.

Jindal, K.B., *A History of Hindi Literature*, New Delhi: Munshiram Manoharlal, 1993.

Joshi, Esha B., ed., *Uttar Pradesh District Gazetteer: Lucknow (India)*, vol. 2, Allahabad: Indian Press Ltd., 1960.

Jotwani, Motilal, *Sufis of Sindh*, Delhi: Govt. of India, 1986.

Kalidasa, *Raghuvaṁśa*, Introduction by H.D. Velankar, Bombay: Nirnaya Sagar Press, 1948.

Kamal al-Din, Ismail, *Persian Poetry, 747–1500: Bibliography*, Kirman: Kitabshinai-i Khvaju, Markaz-i Kirmanshinasi, 1991.

Kamal, Radha, *Theory and Art of Mysticism*, Bombay: Asia Publishing House, 1960.

Karimi-Hakkak, Ahmad, *The Shahnameh of Firdawsi in France and England 1779–1860: A Study of the European Response to the Persian Epic of Kings*, New Jersey: Rutgers, 1979.

Katre, S.M. and P.K. Gode, *Introduction to Indian Textual Criticism*, Poona: Deccan College, 1956.

Kaviraj, Visvanath, *Sāhityadarpaṇa*, Calcutta: Ray Publications, 1957.

Keith, A.B., *A History of Sanskrit Literature*, Oxford: Clarendon Press, 1928.

Kellogg, S.H., *A Grammar of the Hindi Language*, London: Routledge and Kegan Paul, 1955.

Kelly, Margorie, ed., *Islam*, New York: Preager, 1984.

Khan, G.U., ed., *Mainā Satwantī of Ghawwāsi*, Hyderabad: Ilyas Traders, 1981.

Kirmani, W., ed., *Dreams Forgotten: An Anthology of Indo-Persian Poetry*, Aligarh: Aligarh Muslim University Press, 1984.

Kulke, Hermann and Deitmar Rothermund, *A History of India*, London: Routledge, 1992.

Kumari, P., *Padmāvat aur Madhumālatī ke sandarbh meṁ Jāyasī aur Manjhan kā Tulanātmaka Adhyayana*, Meerut: Anu Pustaka, 1986.

Lala, Jayabahadur, *Sufi Sant Sāhitya kā Udbhawa aur Vikās*, Lucknow: Navayug Granthagar, 1969.

Lamb, H., *Omar Khayyam*, North Hollywood: Leisure Books, 1971.

Lambton, Ann K.S., *Persian Grammar*, Cambridge: Cambridge University Press, 1960.

Levy, Reuben, *An Introduction to Persian Literature*, New York: Columbia University Press, 1969.

Lawrence, Bruce B., *Notes from a Distant Flute: The Extant Literature of Pre-Mughal Indian Sufism*, Tehran: Imperial Iranian Academy of Philosophy, 1978.

Levy, Reuben, *An Introduction to Persian Literature*, New York: Columbia University Press, 1969.

Lewisohn, Leonard, *The Legacy of Medieval Persian Sufism*, London, New York: Khaniqahi Nimatullahi Publications, 1993.

———, *Classical Persian Sufism: From its Origin to Rumi*, London, New York: Khaniqahi Nimatullahi Publications, 1993.

Mahesh, Maheshvari Sinha, *The Historical Development of Medieval Hindi Prosody*, Bhagalpur: Bhagalpur University, 1964.

Mardrus and Mathers, eds., *The Thousand Nights and One Night*. Yugoslavia: Dorset Press, 1987.

Mathur, R., *Padumavati: An Etymological Study*, Delhi: National Publishing House, 1974.

Matthews, D.J. and C. Shackle, *An Anthology of Classical Urdu Love Lyrics*, London: Oxford University Press, 1972.

Mayne, Peter, *Saints of Sind*, London: John Murray, 1956.

Mazahri, Ali Muhamma, ed., *Buzurgan-i-Din*, Lahore: Al Faisal Nasherano Tajeran Kutub, 1989.

McGregor, R.S., *A History of Hindi Literature from its Beginnings to the Nineteenth Century*, Wiesbaden: Otto Harrassowitz, 1984.

———, *The Oxford Hindi-English Dictionary*, Oxford: Oxford University Press, 1993.

Mishra, Hridayesh and Shivalochan Pandey, *Hindī-Sāhitya kā Itihāsa*, Patna: Tara Mudrak, 1967.

Mishra, Lakshmikant, *Tulasī aur Jāyasī kī bhāṣā kā Tulanātmaka Adhyayana*, Delhi: Tulika Prakashan, 1991.

Mishra, Maya, *Hindi Sufi Kāvya me Samanvaya Bhāvanā*, New Delhi. Radha Publications, 1962.

Mishra, Ram Prasad, *An Outline of the History of Hindi Literature*, Delhi: Sangita Printers, 1982.

Moayyad, Heshmat, 'Lyric Poetry', in *Persian Literature*, ed. Ehsan Yarshater, New York: Columbia University Press, 1987.

Monier-Williams, *A Sanskrit-English Dictionary*, Delhi: Marwah Publications, rpt., 1986.

Morrison, George, ed., *History of Persian Literature from the Beginning of the Islamic Period to the Present Day*, Leiden: E.J. Brill, 1981.

Muhammad, A., *Awadhī ke bemisāl shāir Malik Muhammad Jāisī kī lājavāb tasnīf Padmāvat kī mukhtasar farhang*, Nindlur: Idarah-i-al Makhdum, 1972.

Mujeeb, M., *Indian Muslims*, New Delhi: Munshiram Manoharlal, 1985.

Mustafa, Hafiz, *Religious Trends in Pre-Islamic Arabic Poetry*, Aligarh: Aligarh Muslim University Press, 1968.

Nagendra, Dr., *Śodha aur Siddhānta*, Delhi: National Publishing House, 1979.

Narang, Gopichand, *Amīr Khusrau ka Hindawī Kāvya*, Delhi: Simanta Prakashan, 1990.

Narang, I., *Jāyasīkṛta Padmāvata kā Anuśīlana: Padmāvatsāra*, Allahabad: Lokabharati Prakashan, 1989.

Nathan, R.S., ed., *Symbolism in Hinduism*, Bombay: Central Chinmaya Mission Trust, 1983.

Nehemia, L., *Conversion to Islam*, New York: Holmes and Meier, 1979.

Neuman, D.M., *The Life of Music in North India*, Detroit: Wayne State University Press, 1980.

Nicholson, R.A., *The Mystics of Islam*, London: Arkana, 1920.

———, ed., *Studies in Islamic Mysticism*, Cambridge: Cambridge University Press, 1921.

———, ed., *Masnavī*, Cambridge: University Printing House, 1934.

———, *Tales of Mystic Meaning*, London: Chapman and Hall Ltd., 1938.

———, ed., *Kashaf al-Mahjub: The Oldest Persian Treatise on Sufism*, Lahore: Islamic Book Foundation, 1976.

———, ed., *Masnavī*, 2 vols., London: Luzac, 1977(a).

———, ed., *Mathnavi of Jalalu'ddin Rumi*, 4 vols., Cambridge: University Printing House, 1977(b).

Nizami, Ganjavi (1140–1202), *Laili wa Majnoun*, ed. Barat Zanjani, Tehran: Publication de L'Universite de Tehran, 1990.

———, *Kulliyat-i-Nizami Ganjavi*, ed. and trans. Dastagardi Vahid, 2 vols., Tehran: Intisharat-i-Nigah, 1993.

Nizami, Khaliq A., ed., *Duwal Rani Khazir Khan*, Delhi: Idarah-i Adabiyat-i Delhi, 1988.

O'Flaherty, W.D., *Hindu Myths*, London: Penguin, 1975.

Onder, Mehmed, *Mevlana and the Mevlana Museum*, Istanbul: Aksit Culture and Tourism Publications, 1985.

Padma, Sudhi, *Symbols of Art, Religion and Philosophy*, New Delhi: Intellectual Publishing House, 1988.

Pandey, Chandra Bali, *Tasawwuf athavā Sūfimat*, Varanasi: Saraswati Mandir, 1966.

Pandey, S.M., *Sūfī Kāvya Vimarśa*, Agra: Vinod Pustak Mandir, 1968.

———, *Hindī aur Fārsī Sūfī Kāvya*, Allahabad: Sahitya Bhawan, 1974.

———, *The Hindi Oral Epic Loriki (The Tale of Lorik and Cāndā)*, Allahabad: Sahitya Bhawan, 1979.

———, *Madhya Yugīna Premākhyāna*, Allahabad: Lok Bharati Prakashan, 1982.

Pandey, Sarojani, *Hindī Sūfī Kāvya meṁ Pratīka Yojanā*, Kanpur: Yugavani Prakashan, 1974.

Parvez, *Tasawwuf kī Haqīqat*, Lahore: Tulu Islam Trust, 1980.

Parveen, Shahnaz, *Cāndāyan kā Sānskṛtik Adhyayana*, New Delhi: Mangala Prakashan, 1985.

Pathak, Sivasahay, *Hindī Sūfī Kāvya kā Samagra Anuśīlana*, New Delhi: Rajkamal Prakashan, 1978.

Peters, F.E., *A Reader on Classical Islam*, Princeton: Princeton University Press, 1994.

Pinto, Desiderio, *Piri-Muridi Relationship: A Study of the Nizamuddin Dargah*, New Delhi: Manohar, 1995, rpt. 2006.

Prasad, R.C., ed., *Rāmacarit of Tulsidas*, Delhi: Motilal Banarsidass, 1978.

Prasad, Shivanandan, *Mātrika Chandoṁ kā Vikāsa*, Patna: Bihar Rastrabhasha Parishad, 1964.

Prasad, Vishvanath, *Cāndāyan*, Agra: Agra University Press, 1962.

Preminger, A. and T.V.F. Brogan, eds., *Princeton Encyclopedia of Poetry and Poetics*, Princeton: Princeton University Press, 1993.

Pritchett, F.W. and K.A. Khaliq, *Urdu Meter*, Madison: University of Wisconsin, Madison Publication Series, 1987.

Puṣpadanta, *Ṇāyakumāracariu*, ed. Hiralal Jain, Benares: Bharatiya Jnanapitha Prakashan, 1944.

Qureshi, Regula Burckhardt, *Sufi Music of India and Pakistan*, Cambridge: Cambridge University Press, 1986.

Raghavan, V. and Nagendra, *An Introduction to Indian Poetics*, Madras: Macmillan, 1970.

Randhawa, M.S., *Indian Miniature Painting*, New Delhi: Roli Books International, 1981.

Ranking, George S.A., ed., *Muntakhab ut-Tawarikh*, 3 vols., Karachi: Karimsons, 1976.

Rizvi, S.A.A., *A History of Sufism in India*, 2 vols., New Delhi: Munshiram Manoharlal, 1975.

Ross, J., ed., *Gulistan of Shaikh Sadi*, Shiraz: Marefat Bookseller and Publisher, 1923.

Rumi, Jalaluddin, *Masnavī*, rpt, Peshawar: Noorani Kutubkhana, 1977.

Sadafi, Aliraza, *Tarh-i-urūz-i-Fārasī*, Tehran: Sazman Intesharat Faruhar, 1979.

Sadiq, Muhammad, *History of Classical Urdu Literature*, London: Oxford University Press, 1964.

Said, E.W., *Orientalism*, New York: Random House, 1979.

———, *Covering Islam*, New York: Pantheon Books, 1981.

Saksena, Baburam, *Evolution of Awadhi (A branch of Hindi)*, Delhi: Motilal Banarsidass, 1971.

Saksena, Sudha, *Jāyasī kī Bimba Yojanā*, Delhi: Ashok Printing Press, 1966.

Salomon, Richard, ed. and trans., *The Bridge to the Three Holy Cities: the Sāmānya-praghattaka of Nārāyaṇa Bhaṭṭa's Tristhalisetu*, Delhi: Motilal Banarsidass, 1985.

Sarkar, J.N., 'A Study of Sufism, Its Background and Syncretic Significance in Medieval India', *Indo-Iranica*, vol. 38, 1985.

Schimmel, A., *Mystical Dimensions of Islam*, Chapel Hill: University of North Carolina Press, 1975.

———, 'Persian Poetry in the Indo-Pakistan Subcontinent', in *Persian Literature Outside Iran*, Calcutta: Bibliotheca Persica, vol. 3, 1985.

———, *Mirror of an Eastern Moon*, London: East-West Publications, 1978.

———, *I am Wind, You Are Fire: The Life and Work of Rumi*, Boston: Shambhala, 1992(a).

———, *Islam: An Introduction*, Albany: State University of New York Press, 1992(b).

———, *The Triumphal Son: A Study of the Works of Jalaluddin Rumi*, Albany: State University of New York Press, 1993.

———, *Deciphering the Signs of God: A Phenomenological Approach to Islam*, Albany: State University of New York Press, 1994.

Schomer, K. and W.H. McLeod, *The Sants: Studies in a Devotional Tradition of India*, Delhi: Motilal Banarsidass, 1987.

Shackle, C., *A Manual of Urdu Metre*, London: School of Oriental and African Studies, 1988.

Shah, A., ed., *The Tales of the Four Dervishes and Other Sufi Tales Retold by Amina Shah*, San Francisco: Harper and Row, 1981.

Shakoor, M., *The Writing on the Water*, Worcester: Billings, Hylton, 1988.

Sharan, Shree and A.M. Rastogi, *Hindī Sāhitya kā Itihās*, Delhi: Prem Prakashan Mandir, 1988.

Sharma, C.A., *A Critical Survey of Indian Philosophy*, Delhi: Motilal Banarsidass, 1964.

Sharma, M.R., *Padmāvatī*, Bhopal: Madhya Pradesh Hindi Granth Academy, 1971.

Sharma, Gyan C., *Cāndāyan kā Sāṁskṛtik Pariveś*, Patiala: Vishal Prakashan, 1973.

Sharma, Rajnath, *Jāyasī Granthāvalī*, Agra: Vinod Pustak Mandir, 1975.

———, *Jāyasī aur unkā Padmāvat: Ek Sarvekṣaṇa*, Agra: Vinod Pustak Mandir, 1962.

Sharma, Rajkumar, *Jāyasī aur unkā Padmāvat*, Jaipur: Padam Book Company, 1967.

Sharma, Vinod Chandra, ed., *District Gazetteer: Faizabad*, no. 37, Allahabad: Job Printers, 1959.

Shastri, Omprakash, *Kāvyālocan*, Delhi: Arya Book Depot, 1967.

Shirani, Mahmood, *Tanqīd bar Āb-i-Hayāt*, in *Oriental College Magazine*, vol. 17, no. 4, 1941.

Shuja'at, S.A., *Amīr Khusrau aur unkī Hindī Kavitā*, Lucknow: Kalabhawan Mudran, 1986.

Shukla, R.C., *Hindi Sāhitya kā Itihās*, Kashi: Nagari Pracharini Sabha, 1965.

Singh, Bachchan, *Ācārya Śukla kā Itihās paṛhte hue*, New Delhi: National Publishing House, 1989.

Sireham, Mahendranath, *Hindu Mysticism According to the Upanisads*, New Delhi: Munshiram Manoharlal, 1974.

Spear, Percival, *A History of India*, 2 vols., New York: Penguin, 1970.

Stetkevych, Susan, ed., *Reorientations: Arabic and Persian Poetry*, Bloomington: Indiana University Press, 1994.

Stetkevych, Pinckney and Susan, eds., *Reorientations: Arabic and Persian Poetry*, Bloomington: Indiana University Press, 1994.

Sūrdāsa, *Sūr Sāgar*, ed. Nand Dulare Vajpeyi, Kashi: Nagari Pracharini Sabha, 1965.

Tabatabai, M.H., *The Quran in Islam*, London: Routledge & Kegan Paul, 1987.

Tanselle, Thomas G., *A Rationale of Textual Criticism*, Philadelphia: University of Pennsylvania Press, 1987.

Thapar, R., *A History of India*, vol. 1, New York: Viking Penguin, 1966.

Tiwari, Bhala Chandra, *Sūfi Kāvya meṁ Nārī*, Lucknow: Sabbarwal Printing Press, 1936.

Tiwari, Bholanath, *Amir Khusrau aur unka Sahitya*, Delhi: Bharat Prakashan, 1985.

———, Nurnabi Abbasi and Kiran Bala, eds., *Bṛhat Hindī Lokokti Kośa*, Delhi: Shan Printers, 1985.

Tripathi, Vidyadhar, *Jāyasī ke Sāhitya meṁ Aprastuta Yojanā*, Mathura: Rajya Shree Prakashan, 1978.

Valiuddin, Mir, *The Quranic Sufism*, Delhi: Motilal Banarsidass, 1977.

Velankar, H.D., 'Apabhraṁśa Metres', *Journal of the University of Bombay*, 2.3, 1933.

———, ed., *Kālidāsa's Raghuvaṁśa*, Bombay: Nirnaya Sagar Press, 1948.

Vyas, Bhola Shankar, ed., *Prākṛta Paiṁgalam*, 2 vols., Benares, 1959–62.

Walker, Benjamin, *Hindu World: An Encyclopedic Survey of Hinduism*, 2 vols., New Delhi: Munshiram Manoharlal, 1983.

Weightman, S.C.R., *Symmetry and Symbolism in Shaik Manjhan's Madhumālatī*, London: School of Oriental and African Studies, 1992.

Wilson, C.E., ed., *The Masnavī*, Karachi: Indus Publications, 1976.

Winternitz, Maurice, *A History of Indian Literature*, 3 vols., Delhi: Motilal Banarsidass, 1981.

Wolpert, S.A., *A New History of India*, New York: Oxford University Press, 1993.

Yarshater, Ehsan, ed., *Lyric Poetry, Persian Literature*, New York: Columbia University Press, 1987.

Zaehner, R.C., *Hindu and Muslim Mysticism*, London: University of London and Athlon Press, 1960.

———, ed., *Hindu Scriptures Selected, Translated and Introduced by R.C. Zaehner*, London: Dent, 1966.

Zaidi, A.J., *A History of Urdu Literature*, New Delhi: Sahitya Akademi, 1993.

Index